生态农业六次产业化

新时代科技特派员创新创业

张来武 著

社会科学文献出版社
SOCIAL SCIENCES ACADEMIC PRESS (CHINA)

图书在版编目（CIP）数据

生态农业六次产业化：新时代科技特派员创新创业 /
张来武著 . -- 北京：社会科学文献出版社, 2024. 9.
ISBN 978-7-5228-3847-2

Ⅰ . F323.2
中国国家版本馆 CIP 数据核字第 2024ED2170 号

生态农业六次产业化：新时代科技特派员创新创业

著　　者 / 张来武

出 版 人 / 冀祥德
组稿编辑 / 恽　薇
责任编辑 / 孔庆梅　欧阳耀福
责任印制 / 王京美

出　　版 / 社会科学文献出版社·经济与管理分社（010）59367226
　　　　　　地址：北京市北三环中路甲29号院华龙大厦　邮编：100029
　　　　　　网址：www.ssap.com.cn
发　　行 / 社会科学文献出版社（010）59367028
印　　装 / 三河市东方印刷有限公司

规　　格 / 开本：889mm×1194mm　1/32
　　　　　　印张：9　字数：210 千字
版　　次 / 2024年9月第1版　2024年9月第1次印刷
书　　号 / ISBN 978-7-5228-3847-2
定　　价 / 79. 00元

读者服务电话：4008918866

序　言

　　我的六次产业理论第一本专著《六次产业理论与创新驱动发展》（2018年，人民出版社）自问世以来，受到社会各界的广泛关注。近年来，正值人类社会经历前所未有的不平凡岁月。新冠疫情的惊涛骇浪，中美博弈以及全球化停滞不前，ChatGPT的横空出世，生成式人工智能（GAI）带来永生与毁灭的无限潜能，无一不表明人类社会已进入数字经济社会的新时代。这个时代需要发展六次产业理论。

　　六次产业理论不仅指引农业六次产业化，还成为全社会数字经济的创新理论。它不仅是从三次产业划分到六次产业划分的产业经济学的突破，也是数字创新和文化创意驱动的创新经济学。六次产业理论的贡献在于四个创新之处，即"四新"：新理论、新要素、新主流和新模式。第一"新"，新理论是新时代的创新理论，这个数字新时代不同于工业经济时代，它的生产函数由于创新太快已不能固定，创新的规律已不再由线性创新理论所刻画。我们提出科学、技术、市场应用三螺旋驱动发展的创新理论（以下简称三螺旋创新理论），在数据驱动的新范式下，螺旋即运算，由此决定系统模式，如第六产业即生态产业的生态模式的运营发展，这是新理论的基石。第二"新"，数据是数字经济中出现的"新生产要素"，这个要素不同于以往经济系统的三要素（劳动、资本和土地），具有替代性、共享性和智能性，这将凸显数字生态的融合与共享特征。第三"新"，新主流是指区别于工业经济的"产品及服务"，而是满足人的情感、梦想和精神需求，它通过文化创意即第五产业满足用户体验价值来实现。第四"新"，由生态链群（联合体）通过基于区块链和智能合约打造新商业模式，即"生态模式"。它与基于核心产品及服务能力的工业模式一起构成共生模式，从而形成双环状系统价值。六次产业理论指引人类社会从工业化走向六次产业化，其本质可以概括为一个基本公式：六次产业化＝数字化⊕生态化，这里的"⊕"就是系统的运算。

随着六次产业理论的创建和深入发展，互联网平台企业等数据产业（第四产业）、基于文化创意的智慧产业（第五产业）和基于融合与共享的生态产业（第六产业）如雨后春笋般破土而出。大量案例的创始人并不了解六次产业理论，作为实战者虽已获得了阶段性成功，但缺乏理论指导，免不了要经历黑暗中的苦苦探索，有的不可持续，甚至陷入深坑而失败。李子柒、董宇辉等的成功、挫折与再生，"村超"与中超的比肩与反差，淄博烧烤的流量带动的文化创意启迪，蚂蚁金服的成功与挫折，腾讯的成功及与抖音不合作博弈中的遗憾，元宇宙经济带来的惊异和迷茫等都能用六次产业理论进行很好的解释。值得特别关注的案例是海尔和滴灌通。海尔在其创始人张瑞敏先生带领下，破除了互联网平台发展中的工业化思维，创造了"人单合一"的生态模式。海尔独具数字化和生态化创新的双向努力。另一个重要案例是滴灌通。其核心产品每日收入分成合约（DRC）是国内首个以收入分成模式服务于小微企业的融资，而其成败的关键在于每日收入分成凭证（DRO）的交易背后的逻辑是不是数字化生态化（六次产业化）的链群结构。在与滴灌通CEO张高波、首席风险官邓晓力女士进行数十次交流后，我更加确信滴灌通的发展将取决于生态金融的持续创新。上述案例都说明六次产业理论的发展与实践创新的及时互动是非常重要的。由此我们选择六次产业理论对话录的形式出版，以便以新媒体方式快速传播，这更有利于推动六次产业化实践。

六次产业理论对话录拟为系列丛书。从生态农业六次产业化开始，还将不定期陆续出版未来产业对话录、医疗健康六次产业化对话录、生态金融六次产业化对话录、数据产业对话录、文化创意产业对话录、生态经济对话录等。对于第一本对话录，我们选择以农业为对象，这是推动新时代科技特派员创新创业、贯彻党中央乡村振兴大政方针的需要，也是基于六次产业化的城乡一体化发展的战略机遇，根治中国城乡二元结构问题的选择。这样的选择既有战略性考量，也有可行性考量。发展农业六产，选择聚焦生态农业六次产业化，依托科技特派员制度和网络，推动专项行动是基于六次产业理论的历史演进：先有农业六次产业化，后有六次产业理论，而农业六次产业化的两个实践来源是日本农业六次产业化和中国科技特派员制度。因此，第一本对话录的名称为《生态农业六次产业化：新时代科技特派员创新创业》，旨在通过生态农业六次产业化，推动新时代科技特派员创新创业。

中国科技特派员制度发端于 1999 年的福建南平，2001年结合宁夏提出的"科技创业行动"，共同形成了"科技特派员基层创业行动"（南平经验和宁夏模式）。而后浙江、江苏、山东、新疆、广东、海南等地又进行了实践创新。经过20 多年的发展，中国科技特派员已有百万大军，形成了全国范围内的社会化网络，获得各地区各级政府的指导和支持，并于 2016 年由国务院发布文件形成制度。

科技特派员创新创业在中国脱贫攻坚阶段发挥了重要作用，得到习近平总书记的充分肯定，也受到联合国的高度关注，并在国际扶贫行动中加以推广。在进入数字化新时代，科技特派员创新创业进入了乡村振兴的新阶段，需要与时俱进，实行基于数字化生态化（六次产业化）的制度创新、科技创新和模式创新，这就是六次产业理论对话录的宗旨。

首本对话录总共六章：第一章，揭示什么是六次产业理论及其重要应用、六次产业化与工业化有什么区别；第二章，在学理层面，讨论农业六次产业理论和在乡村振兴下的生态农业六次产业化的逻辑；第三章，在实践层面，讨论如何培育、设计生态模式，推动农业六次产业化；第四章，讨论科技特派员制度的历史、典型模式以及演化历程；第五章，讨论科技特派员如何利用数据新要素、新平台开展创新创业；第六章，讨论围绕用户体验价值的高附加值的第五产业及第六产业运作的逻辑与现实案例，给科技特派员创新创业提供新的启迪、思路和动能。

在对话录形成过程中，对话录的问题设计和回答基于我所做的总体结构安排和多年来的会议演讲报告。对一些关键章节和问题，我和我的对话录创作团队成员进行了深入讨论。在具体行文上，复旦大学六次产业研究院的诸位老师、博士后和研究院外的一些专家做了重要的贡献，因此，这本对话录也是集体创作的成果。对话录团队成员的贡献如下：楼国强副教授整理第一章的文稿；王小林教授整理第二章、第三章的文稿；第四章的文稿先由珠海（横琴）食品安全研究院的袁学国副院长整理，之后由王小林教授和张晓颖青年副研究员做了大量补充，并由王小林教授修订；第五章的文稿由冯贺霞研究员和王小林教授共同整理和修订；第六章的文稿由郎有泽青年副研究员、楼国强副教授共同整理和修订。除此之外，研究院的博士后李夏伟、李明圆以及《环球财经》记者刘霄霞共同参与了讨论，刘霄霞记者还参与全书的文字校对。此外，为了更好地进行国际交流传播，我们采取了中英文双语版本。

最后，感谢西北农林科技大学六次产业研究院、杨凌第六产业研究中心创新研究院和珠海（横琴）食品安全研究院（国家食品安全创新工程中心秘书处）作为生态农业六次产业化专项行动的发起方率先推动生态农业六次产业化。要特别致谢的发起方的专家教授有：张光强、赵敏娟、钱永华、吴忠、胡京华、夏显力、余劲、钱立、张庆武等。我们也非常期待六次产业理论发展和实践创新领军人才辈出，形成高水平的团队，不断续写六次产业理论对话录新篇章。

目　录

第一章　六次产业理论对话录

问题 1：什么是六次产业理论？

随着人类从农业社会进入工业社会，新西兰经济学家费歇尔（Fisher）和英国经济学家克拉克（Clarke）总结产业发展规律，按劳动对象把产业划分为三次产业：将获取自然资源的产业划为第一产业；将加工自然资源以及对加工过的产品进行再加工的产业划为第二产业；将第一、第二产业之外的所有产业，如服务业，都划为第三产业。

2023 年，中国信息通信研究院发布的《中国数字经济发展研究报告（2023 年）》显示，2022 年，我国数字经济规模达到 50.2 万亿元，占 GDP 的比重为 41.5%。我国经济正在从工业经济蝶变到数字经济，并涌现出消费的新主流、生产的新要素、产业的新业态。因此产生了不能由传统产业模式所包容的新产业形态，即经营数据的第四产业、经营用户体验价值的第五产业以及形成生态模式的跨界融合的第六产业。在这样的时代背景下，六次产业理论应运而生。

传统的三次产业理论在工业化背景下强调分工与竞争，形成以"物"为本的产业规律，而六次产业理论则不同。六次产业理论强调融合与共享，形成以"人"为本的产业规律。六次产业理论首先从数字经济时代的产业经济学突破开始，探索了数字时代的创新理论，从线性创新理论出发发展了三螺旋创新理论。

问题 2：六次产业理论作为数字时代创新经济学，具有哪些突破性理论贡献？

六次产业理论的突破性理论贡献可以概括为"四新"：第一，"新理论"，六次产业理论是数字经济时代的创新理论；第二，"新要素"，六次产业理论认为数据（涉及第四产业）是数字经济时代的"新要素"，这一要素催生新的生产力和生产关系；第三，"新主流"，六次产业理论深入研究"新主流"的价值创造，与传统的理论强调供给的"物"不同，该理论强调"人"，第五产业的文化创意从用户体验价值来构造商业价值；第四，"新模式"，新旧生产要素跨产业融合形成第六产业，并产生"新模式"即生态模式。新时代中的产业发展基于股权激励，关注专业化和分工体系，而第六产业则更关注融合创新，基于商业生态系统的链群，通过智能合约来实现跨界的价值创造与分享。

数字经济是继农业经济、工业经济后出现的新经济形态。为大家所熟知的摩尔定律，指出电脑性能每 18 个月翻一番。因此，数字经济的创新无法用生产函数来固定，无法用传统的最优化理论解释，它颠覆了传统经济学的基础。2023 年诞生的 ChatGPT，让我们见到了生成式人工智能的巨大威力。数字经济带来了通用技术的重大变革，而这必然会带来经济模式的深刻变化。变革的核心在于创新模式发生了重大突破。在工业化社会中，耳熟能详的创新模式是线性创新模式，它最初是由万尼瓦尔·布什（Vannevar Bush）在 1945 年提出的，是理解科学技术与经济关系的一个理论框架。该模式假定创新从基础研究开始，到应用研究展开，最后以生产和扩散结束。如果创新是线性的，那么政府可以设计创新过程，而现实中这往往导致低效。基于六次产业理论，我们提出了三螺旋创新理论，科学、技术和市场应用在复杂系统中以一种螺旋的方式相互作用和发展。科学和技术是两个不同的螺旋。科学史告诉我们，很久以来，科学和技术是几乎完全独立的，比如中国四大发明是在实践经验基础上产生的。科学和技术是到了近代，特别是科学革命之后才逐渐结合在一起的。两者的发展逻辑不同，科学是科学家出于对自然世界的好奇心驱动探索并不断积累发展的知识，技术则是针对实际问题而提供的解决方案。对于市场应用来说，科学和技术可以用不同的路径发挥作用。科学，有时不需要通过技术转化，而直接进入市场应用场景，以区块链为例，密码学、博弈论的激励机制设计直接进入区块链系统中。在数字经济中，各种形式的数据进入应用的过程需要更多跨学科的科学知识与技术融合，比如在精准医学中，生命科学与信息技术（生成式人工智能）的融合运用更是发挥重要作用。科学、技术与应用场景的三螺旋推动数字经济中产业新业态的形成。

数据是数字经济中新的生产要素，数据驱动与数据经营的新业态属于第四产业。数据，作为生产要素，有一些基本特性。第一，替代性，数据要素在供给体系中可以替代传统生产要素，比如资产与劳动力。第二，智能性，数据只有通过知识体系的构建，通过人以及人工智能的结合才能进入生产体系。在数字经济中，存在三类知识体系，即明知识、默知识和暗知识。明知识既可意会又能言传，比如一些操作流程的知识；默知识，只可意会不可言传，比如企业家对市场机会的认知；暗知识，既不可意会也不能言传，只能通过人工智能和机器来解读，比如各种 0-1 代码。在数字社会中，这种知识对于经济运行发挥越来越大的作用。在前些年，DeepMind 开发的 AlphaGo 打败了人类围棋顶尖高手，而之后基于不同范式开发的阿尔法零则通过自我学习算法，碾压并完胜 AlphaGo。2023 年，横空出世的 ChatGPT 通过以大规模数据为基础的生成式人工智能惊艳世界。人们传统认识中一些机器智能的天花板领域、需要创意的领域，如数学证明，已经开始被人工智能渗透。第三，共享性，数据不共享意味着会出现信息孤岛，数据不流通就发挥不了数据对传统产业的变革影响。数据驱动的产业模式，不仅改变了生产，也改变了商业模式。对于平台经济、区块链、元宇宙等新业态，已经无法使用传统三次产业理论来解释其产业逻辑。平台经济与传统的基于产品和服务的商业模式大相径庭，我们会看到消费者有时候可以无偿，甚至有补贴地获得服务。在资本市场中，对数字企业的价值评估不再基于传统财务收益而基于"市售率"甚至"市梦率"等。这些新的产业现象无法依据传统三次产业理论划分，而是一种数字经济时代出现的全新的业态。

第五产业，又称智慧产业，它是基于社会上新的消费主流而诞生的新产业形态。丹麦未来学家沃尔夫·伦森指出，人类在经历狩猎社会、农业社会、工业社会和信息社会之后，将进入一个以关注梦想、历险、精神及情感生活为特征的梦想社会，人们消费的注意力将主要转移到精神文化的需求上。第五产业是以数字化为基础，经营用户体验价值的新业态。与传统产业侧重于商品和服务不同，第五产业的核心是用户的体验价值。第五产业作为经营体验价值的产业，利用数字化技术体系，打通了消费与生产的界限。消费者主动参与到生产供应的设计之中，通过数据来进行个性化的体验设计。尽管在工业化社会中也存在文化创意产业，然而由于没有数字化的基础，这种个性化设计的成本通常会相当高，文化创意与产业的结合往往带有工业化痕迹，在市场上提供的服务是高度相似的。比如，在许多乡村文化旅游产业中，大多乡村的设计千篇一律。元宇宙是典型的第五产业案例，是在数字化的虚拟世界中，针对不同用户经营个性化的体验价值的产业链。如果说微信带来以语音为载体的社群文化交流体验，抖音能够提供以短视频为载体的个性化表达的体验，在元宇宙中，满足人们各式各样精神文化的体验价值的产业将涌现。第五产业在经营体验价值中，往往需要打通产业链和价值链，打造体验价值的跨产业生态模式，这就成为商业生态圈的基础。

第六产业以共享知识和技术体系为基础，围绕消费者体验价值而对跨产业系统经营形成商业生态系统。第六产业本质上是（商业）生态经济模式。在第六产业中，存在从内到外的多层商业圈，内圈基于产业分工的传统行业供给技术能力来获得收益，中间圈是基于某类消费者体验价值而建构的跨产业子生态圈，外圈则是基于用户关联的动态的价值体验形成的子生态圈联盟而形成的大生态圈或商业链群。在第六产业中，在生态圈内部是基于合作而形成的联盟。与此同时，不同生态圈之间存在竞争。在第六产业的商业圈中，为激励不同形式和层次的合作，需要形成一个基于贡献的利益分享机制。固定模式的传统股权结构往往不能（灵活地）适应这种来自跨界动态的价值分配，越来越多的商业生态系统基于链群的价值合作分享机制来动态实现。从第六产业的视角来看，我们可以解释在软件行业中出现的基于共享形态的架构，比如开源体系。

六次产业理论是基于上文"四新"形成的数字经济的创新理论，其本质可以概括为一个基本公式：六次产业化 = 数字化 $\oplus$ 生态化。"$\oplus$" 不是单纯的组合叠加，而是系统的运算，这种运算可以来自多种方式，包括生成式人工智能和区块链。

问题 3：什么是生态经济模式？它与工业经济模式的区别是什么？它对现实有什么指导意义？

六次产业理论的生态经济模式，不仅包括自然生态，还包括社会生态、商业生态等。与工业经济相比，生态经济存在三个本质区别。

第一，产业的核心对象不同。对于工业经济来说，产品和服务是核心。从工业革命开始以来，工业化相比农业社会提供了成本更低的商品（最初是纺织品），以及更高质量的商品和服务，企业的核心竞争力在于商品的成本较低或者质量超越对手。然而，在生态经济模式中，核心对象不再是产品和服务，而是用户体验价值。尽管说用户体验价值会依赖产品或服务的实体，但是其本质发生了很大变化。生态经济模式不是先生产产品再去市场上销售，而是先寻找用户的体验价值再来设计企业或者企业联盟需要的产品和服务。用户体验价值的商业化运营是生态经济的核心对象，比如，未来学派提到的一个商业案例，尽管放养鸡产的蛋与普通鸡蛋在营养成分方面没多大区别，却存在一个明显的价格差距，这个价格差距可能体现了消费者对于动物保护的价值认同。

第二，经营模式不同。在工业经济中，企业是最基本的经营单元，企业通过股权结构界定参与各方的责权利，同时，股权可以在资本市场上交易，通过交易来优化效率。在生态经济中，链群是一个基本经营模式。在经营用户体验价值过程中所需的跨界合作各方，在链群中共同创造价值，同时以贡献为基础，通过智能合约等形式来分配链群合作收益，这一合约又称为链群合约。与股权合约相比，链群合约可以在动态联盟合作过程中，灵活合理地分配合作增量收益，而不是依照事前固定的比例来分配，同时也在一定程度上降低了股权结构形成过程中讨价还价的成本。在链群模式下，一个典型企业有双环账（财务报表）：内环账是传统财务的报表，它基于原先产业通过提供商品和服务而获得的回报；外环账来自生态圈，通过链群合约获得所在的商业生态圈的合作收益。

第三，供需之间关系不同。在传统的工业化模型中，企业生产的商品，通过市场销售到达消费者手中，消费者与生产者是两个独立的群体。在生态经济模型中，由于经营用户体验极其重要，用户全程参与是其中重要的一个环节。很多产业，比如数字医疗，如果不引入用户，单纯依靠病人病历的数据就难以形成数字化服务的基础。在全病程管理以及全健康流程管理中，用户（在生病的阶段成为患者）主动分享数据，系统通过数据汇总和分析动态跟踪用户身体状况的变化，通过对大量用户健康数据的智能训练，可以在其健康状况发生变化时进行诊断，对于治疗以及后续健康管理都能提供一个更准确的个性化方案。在保护用户隐私的基础上，这种信息分享也能给提供者带来收益。此外，与工业经济模式相比，生态经济的特点打破了生产者与消费者的角色壁垒，为用户体验价值的形成创造了基础。

党的十八大以来，中央围绕生态经济提出了一系列新发展理念，如绿色低碳高质量发展，把经济建设与环境保护，特别是与"碳达峰""碳中和"的目标相结合。与此同时，中央为实现巩固拓展脱贫攻坚成果同乡村振兴有效衔接，提出了促进农村产业兴旺等一系列任务目标。六次产业理论中的生态经济可以为贯彻中央的新发展理念提供一些新思路。

首先，乡村振兴战略中的产业兴旺与六次产业理论中的三产融合是相通的。六次产业理论中的产业创新升级有不同于传统产业经济学的新思路、新理论和新方法，其标志就是数字化时代兴起的以互联网产业为代表的诸多新产业，包括数据驱动的"互联网+"产业、用户体验价值驱动的"文化创意+"产业以及以合作共享为基础的生态经济。在产业兴旺的过程中，可以充分发挥在中国有百万之众的科技特派员在基层创新创业中的作用。

其次，在贯彻绿色低碳高质量发展战略中，充分发展生态经济是其中重要的新模式探索。在六次产业理论中，生态经济发展需要两大基石：第一个基石是数据，数据是一个新的生产要素，要经营好数据，发展第四产业；第二个基石是生态社会资本，它来自第五产业的文化创意理念，以及第六产业的共享产业理念。数据基石，是六次产业理论的优势，也是创新时代的一个亮点和转折点。在传统的三次产业理论中，生态往往是经营的成本。生态找不到附加值，没有实现良性循环的机制。在传统的三次产业中，生态环境恶化往往成为进行工业化发展的代价。在数据化转型阶段，如何让生态可以被打造为资本？其核心在于如何通过数据要素把生态代入高附加值的商业模式之中。生态社会资本这个概念首先来自第五产业的范畴。第五产业基于两条线出现：一是科学前沿的创新，科学前沿的发现有时无须通过技术转化直接进入生产；二是文化创意的创新，在后工业化时代，人们的主流需求不只是物质和服务，还有精神、梦想、情感的需求，比如游戏产业、影视产业等。在这样的一个新需求模式下，生态满足了人和自然的良性关系的需求，有益于人类健康，给文明社会带来一种心灵的治愈。文化创意能够逐渐形成生态资本。随着生态资本的积累，我们才能发展第四、第五产业，才能发展共享农业，才能发展具有更高附加值的农业。随着农业六次产业化的发展，生态资本必然会被未来的消费者认可，以及被资本市场认可。

问题 4：六次产业理论与日本六次产业化的
区别是什么？

六次产业理论与日本的六次产业化有很大的区别。日本的农业专家今村奈良臣在 20 世纪 90 年代提出"第六产业是第一、二、三产业相加或相乘"，即通过延长产业链，把农业与工业、服务业融合，增加附加值，来进行产业升级。这一概念影响了日本的农业政策，基于今村奈良臣的农业产业链延长的思路，2008 年，日本提出六次产业化，换句话说就是"接二连三"。日本提出六次产业化有一定的现实基础。首先，日本的农业机械化程度高；其次，日本农协有相当强的组织能力和话语权，能代表农民与大资本谈判。可以说，日本的六次产业化是在工业化社会中，农业经济学的创新。

我们提出六次产业理论，也提出六次产业化的概念，然而，这一概念建立在数字经济时代。六次产业化 = 数字化⊕生态化，这里"⊕"不是单纯的组合叠加，而是系统的运算。与日本的六次产业化相比，我们首先形成了一套数字经济的创新理论，其中包括数字经济的第四、第五和第六产业，这一理论不仅可以应用于农业，也可以应用于其他领域，比如医疗健康、金融、未来科学技术和产业等。

我国的农业六次产业化，除了借鉴日本的六次产业化外，还有一个更基础的本土实践来源，就是中国科技特派员制度。中国科技特派员制度于 1999 年发轫于福建南平，最初是政府推动的农业科技服务，后来科技特派员模式创新则更多的是农村基层创新创业行动。科技特派员经过 20 多年的发展，如今在全国有上百万之众。很多科技特派员纷纷利用数字化的工具、文化创意等方法，推动农村三产融合。

随着中央政府提出巩固拓展脱贫攻坚成果有效衔接乡村振兴，提出绿色低碳高质量发展，中国的农业六次产业化（数字化⊕生态化）将形成一系列新的产业模式和商业模式，如碳汇农业是把农业与碳排放相结合的生态农业，这无不推动对新时代下生态农业六次产业化新的创新落地模式的探索。

问题 5：六次产业理论的典型应用是什么？

在对前面问题的回答中，我们解释了六次产业理论的应用领域超越了农业领域。六次产业理论的典型应用主要有以下四个方面。

第一，生态农业六次产业化。我们在前面提到了碳汇农业是一种融合碳排放、碳金融、碳交易与农业形成的生态产业。在解决中国长期存在的二元经济结构问题、推动乡村产业兴旺的过程中，未来农业将发挥重要作用。未来农业在本质上就是生态农业，它强调通过跨界的产业融合，形成生态圈；通过满足客户的体验价值，来解决农业的低附加值问题。健康农业强调的是农业与健康产业形成生态圈，通过生物科技、信息技术（BT+IT 融合）、医疗健康与农业形成大的商业生态系统，这将有非常大的市场潜力。比如，中医药种植可以与生物科技、信息技术、医疗健康融合形成商业生态系统。文创农业，把精神文化价值与特色农业结合起来，将实现农业的产业升级。比如宁夏的葡萄酒产业，目前已经形成了贺兰山东麓的葡萄种植基地，其逐渐发展成为与世界知名葡萄酒产地法国波尔多、意大利托斯卡纳、美国加利福尼亚州等大产区齐名的种植基地。在实现产业升级中，可以将文化创意与葡萄产业结合，比如（包括虚拟）葡萄酒酒庄、葡萄酒文旅等，开展消费者在葡萄酒与其他体验价值方面的商业策划设计。如此将在更大程度上推动宁夏葡萄酒产业升级，带来更多的基于产业融合的附加值等。未来农业通过数字化⊕生态化的新模式，将为"三农"问题的解决提供一个新的产业发展思路。

第二，医疗健康六次产业化。"看病难、看病贵"的问题让医疗成为新时代人民面临的重要问题。针对这一问题，中央政府出台了许多医改方案，比如医药分离、分级诊疗的医联体，也包括前几年提出的"互联网＋医疗健康"模式等。这些改革的初衷都是为了实现"健康中国"的目标，然而在实践中总会遇到各种障碍。比如，在"互联网＋医疗健康"中，许多医院投入巨资建设信息化系统，然而，这种信息化系统中的各个部分各自为政，数据不共享，形成了一座座医疗信息孤岛。此外，医生在线上诊疗的效率也比线下低，医院的互联网医疗往往成为医生的负担，而且线上诊疗也只能集中于轻问诊环节。微医等互联网公司打造的流量模式的互联网医疗，实质上会与医院抢医生的时间资源，与医院之间很难形成利益相容的生态圈。这两类互联网医疗还是围绕以医院医生为核心，以治病为导向开展的工业化医疗。我们提出了第三类互联网医疗，即研究型互联网医院，与医院、医生形成互补的生态系统，一方面，解决医院无法提供的医疗健康服务问题，比如在全病程管理中除去在医院诊疗的环节，在平时的健康管理以及术后的健康管理中寻找互补的生态空间。另一方面，在保护用户隐私的基础上，通过系统收集来自各个健康阶段的数据进行研究，可以提供个性化的治疗方案，实现科研即服务的目标。在此基础上打造"大健康"，如包括保险在内的更大的生态圈。这一模式，以用户（患者）为核心，围绕用户全病程管理过程的体验价值开展生态系统的打造。目前，该模式已经开始在全国多个地方开展创新试点。

第三，未来产业六次产业化。随着数字技术的不断发展，大数据、云计算、区块链以及生成式人工智能在近些年应运而生，一些新的产业形态如元宇宙也不断涌现。这些新的技术和产业都是数字经济深入发展的产物，这些技术和产业对经济的影响也需要从数字经济的创新经济学视角解读。这些技术和产业绝大多数以数据为驱动因素，有些产业如元宇宙则把用户体验价值作为商业模式核心，而且所有这些技术和产业的发展都离不开打造一个相关的跨界生态圈。

我们以区块链为案例来解读。区块链不是一个单纯的技术或者技术集合，而是一个商业生态系统。我们说先有比特币才有区块链，而不是倒过来，先有应用场景，之后围绕应用场景来打造各种技术和商业的生态圈。由此我们提出的第六产业是区块链发展的主战场。对于区块链，一个又一个区块组成的链条，是否有与其适配的应用场景决定了它能否产生效益。如果没有合适的应用场景，那么区块链只有成本没有效益，只是将技术做得复杂好看，并不实用。第六产业又称共享产业，这意味着它是很多不同产业模块之间连接起来形成的一体化的共享系统，这正好与区块链的组成特点一致。区块链是科学、技术和应用场景三个要素摞在一起形成的螺旋，区块链需要有相关的应用场景，这样才能使核心技术比如智能合约、非对称加密、共识机制等发挥作用。由于区块链具有数据难以篡改和去中心化两大特点，这可以帮助人们解决信任问题，形成合作联盟，而这恰恰是第六产业必须解决的问题。从这个角度来说，区块链从技术上解决了第六产业的共享难题，为其提供了微观经营模式。区块链需要六次产业理论指导，从而解决它的主战场即它的应用场景问题。此外，区块链还营造了文化创意共享的生态。

至于资本市场热炒的元宇宙，在其概念中，数字虚拟世界与现实世界是平行的，它们把工业化时代与数字化时代割裂成两个同时代、分裂的平行世界。这种观点本质上属于工业化视角的观点，基于三次产业理论而非六次产业理论形成。六次产业理论认为大可不必把人类分成两个分裂的平行世界，未来时代发展趋势应该是虚拟世界与现实世界、数字化世界与工业化世界变得越来越融合，越来越紧密。元宇宙是数字化时代发展过程中形成的人类数字化宇宙，元宇宙产业需要从中寻找到满足用户体验价值的商业机会，并由此打造商业生态圈，推动以数字化和生态化方式对新产业业态和商业化模式进行创新。

第四，生态金融六次产业化。生态金融是利用区块链模式以智能合约来打造金融的生态化模式。传统的金融以股权为基础，基于传统财务报告识别一个经营主体未来的现金流，并由此进行定价以及交易。对于一些具有商业盈利能力，但缺乏资本借贷扩张能力的企业，生态金融可以帮助其打造商业生态系统，并在此过程中，协同创造生态圈价值，利用智能合约的方式分享合作收益。目前，一个具有生态金融初步形态的初创企业——滴灌通就是典型例子。滴灌通先从投资小微企业入手，并不形成股权和债权，而是共同创业，通过对于扩张后营业额分成的智能合约直接分配合作收益。经过一段时间的实践检验，这一模式相当成功，目前已有上万个门店品牌进入这一智能合约。这一公司还在一级资本市场澳交所上市，并形成了证券化。这一实践开创了生态金融的先河，当然这一模式的市场生命力还有待时间的进一步检验，但这种用生态模式开创的金融新业态也是新时代的一个重要探索。

第二章　生态农业六次产业化

问题 1：我国农业现代化和乡村振兴面临哪些主要挑战？

习近平总书记表示未来"三农"工作要"全面推进乡村振兴，到 2035 年基本实现农业现代化，到本世纪中叶建成农业强国"[①]。我们的目标与发达国家具有相同性，即保障食物供给，增加农民收入，缩小城乡差距，实现农业农村可持续发展。但是中国国情与发达国家具有差异，中国农业现代化和乡村振兴面临的主要挑战与发达国家不同，应对这些挑战不能生搬硬套国外的理论，而需要遵循我国国情，运用具有中国特色的理论。

第一，中国走的是小农户家庭经营的农业现代化道路。 人多地少，以小农户家庭经营为主，这是我们的基本面。第

---

① 习近平：《加快建设农业强国　推进农业农村现代化》，《求是》2023 年第 6 期。

三次全国农业普查数据显示，全国小农户数量占农业经营主体数量的 98% 以上，户均经营面积规模只有 7.8 亩，小农户经营耕地面积占总耕地面积的 70%。[①] 这样的小农户经营与美国大规模的农场经营完全不同。因此，我们的挑战是在有限的农业资源约束下，提高小农户收入，保障国家粮食安全，缩小城乡发展差距。保障"中国人的饭碗端在自己手里"是我国农业现代化的第一要义。

第二，中国走的是绿色发展的农业现代化道路。人多地少，要提高农业生产率，我们在相当长一段时间走的是增加农业化学投入的路径，即大量投入化肥、农药、化学保鲜剂等。然而，土地退化、土壤污染等，曾经带来严重的食品安全问题。2008 年"毒奶粉"事件发生后，我国的消费者跑到世界各地买奶粉。可以说，食品安全无小事。此外，水污染、空气污染、生物多样性减少，气候变化带来的自然灾害增加，使人们更加注重可持续发展。实践证明，原来的道路不能一直走下去，我们需要一条创新路径，即降低农业的化学投入，保护农业的自然生态。因此，我们面临的挑战是如何通过科技进步，推动中国农业的绿色发展转型。我们要在实现"碳达峰""碳中和"目标的过程中实现农业现代化。而当时美国、欧盟、日本的农业现代化并没有面临"碳达

---

① 《第三次全国农业普查主要数据公报（第一号）》，中国政府网，https://www.gov.cn/xinwen/2017-12/14/content_5246817.htm。

峰""碳中和"的约束。

第三，中国走的是城乡平衡发展的农业现代化道路。区域差距、城乡差距、群体差距是我国实现共同富裕面临的三大差距。我国的城乡差距与发达国家比起来较大，现代化的城市与相对欠发达的农村，形成了相对稳定的二元结构问题，几十年来，我们一直试图破解这个二元结构问题。尽管我国的城市化率已超过 65%，但是对于 14 多亿人口的大国来说，接近 35% 的农村人口仍是相当大的规模。改革开放以来，我国开展脱贫攻坚、乡村振兴工作，目标始终是促进农村繁荣，缩小城乡差距。在工业化、城市化进程中，一方面，将农民转移到城市，进行非农就业；另一方面，部分农民进城落户，为农业现代化和乡村振兴提供了机会。特别是在西部欠发达地区，这三大差距往往交织在一起。因此，在人口老龄化与农村始终承担就业、养老功能的现状下，如何实现乡村振兴是我们需要面对的挑战。

第四，中国走的是数字文明时代的农业现代化道路。无论是美国、欧盟国家还是日本，发达国家的农业现代化伴随着工业化和城市化。与发达国家所走过的农业现代化道路不同，中国当前和今后的农业现代化过程恰逢人类进入数字文明新时代。这个特征使我们有机会利用数据新要素、数字新平台、数据新资产等数字经济的一些优势改造农业、融合农业，创造新的农业现代化道路。也就是说，我们虽然没有美国、欧盟那样的农业条件，但也不是没有出路。数字经济为农业现代化提供了新路径。我们说,生态农业六次产业化的基石就是以数据为新要素,创建农业第四、第五和第六产业新模式,这符合人口主观福利和情感梦想的消费新主流。因此,利用数字文明创造的新技术,开辟乡村产业融合发展、城乡产业融合发展的新道路是我们面临的挑战,也是机遇。

问题 2:什么是生态农业六次产业化?

我们首先来谈谈自然生态、商业生态和社会生态这三个概念,在此基础上,我们再展开讨论什么是生态农业六次产业化,以及为什么说中国农业现代化要走生态农业六次产业化道路。

(一)自然生态、商业生态与社会生态

农业现代化新生态包括乡村产业的自然生态、商业生态和社会生态三个方面。数字化有助于培育农业现代化新生态。

第一,尊重农业的自然生态规律,推进乡村产业全过程绿色转型。自然生态系统是一个由生物和非生物组成的自然群落,它们在自然界中共生存在。自然群落的每个组成部分通过物理、化学和生物过程相互作用。生态系统的每一个要素都是直接或间接相关的,不是相互独立存在的。工业化的发明,对农业生态系统进行干预,以便提高农业生产率。但是,过度干预自然生态系统,也给我们带来食品安全、食源性传染病等诸多问题。因此,我们提出,尊重农业的自然生

态规律，推进乡村产业全过程绿色转型。

党的二十大报告指出，尊重自然、顺应自然、保护自然，是全面建设社会主义现代化国家的内在要求。因此，乡村产业振兴必须牢固树立和践行"绿水青山就是金山银山"的理念，站在人与自然和谐共生的高度谋划。以绿色发展理念为指导，以"碳达峰""碳中和"目标为约束，加快乡村产业发展方式绿色转型是中国农业现代化的必然路径。一是加强农业资源环境保护。强化盐碱化、土壤侵蚀、重金属污染等退化耕地治理。改进农业节水灌溉技术，提高节水效率，降低农业资源利用强度。二是修复农业生态系统，保护农业生物多样性。三是构建绿色低碳乡村产业体系，建立生态产品价值实现机制，完善生态保护补偿制度。事实上，乡村产业的绿色化转型，需要以数字化转型为支撑。碳核算、碳交易、生态价值的实现等都需要把科学精准、易获取、低成本的数据作为基础。

日本索尼计算机科学实验室（Sony Computer Science Laboratories，Sony CSL）研发的一项农业技术，致力于解决环境问题与食品健康、贫困等社会问题，称为"协生农法"。针对只种植单一作物的农业工业化分工所带来的生态环境问题，"协生农法"主张将多种多样的植物以高密度混种，无须耕土、施肥以及喷洒农药，通过不同植物之间，以及农作物与外界的相互作用使农作物达到有序自然生长的状态。"协生农法"有助于解决当今地球上存在的环境恶化、食品品质低下、贫困等社会课题，这将对实现可持续发展目标做出重要贡献。索尼（中国）协同在华企业已经在无锡、惠州、苏州等地开展"协生农法"种植实践。作为 Sony CSL 在生物多样性保护领域开展的创新型举措，"协生农法"及相关实践活动正在持续探索与自然和谐共处、保持生态平衡的可行之道。虽然不能说"协生农法"就一定体现农业的未来，但这个案例为我们提供了一种不同于农业工业化的新思路。

第二，适应数字经济发展规律，构建乡村产业振兴的商业生态。在工业化时代，农业产业化遵从分工与竞争的经济学逻辑。在此过程中，农业处于产业链的上游，附加值低，劳动力投入高。按照发展经济学的"中心－外围"理论，农业凋敝，农村衰落，形成城乡"二元格局"。在数字经济时代，破解这种"二元格局"，需要构建乡村产业的商业生态。商业生态具有以下几个特征。一是从"以农产品为中心"向"以用户终身体验价值为中心"转变。用户价值是数字经济的典型特征，每个平台都在进行用户"数字画像"，期望提高用户体验，增加用户黏性。二是数字经济时代的合作与融合同工业经济时代的分工与竞争共生。相对于工业经济时代，农产品供应链的上下游"供应商合约"，在数字经济时代正迈向"生态合约"或"链群合约"。"生态合约"或"链群合约"不是分工与竞争模式，而是合作与融合模式。生态伙伴、链群伙伴以用户终身价值为中心，共同创造和分享新的价值增值。因此，乡村产业振兴需要把农户和新型农业经营主体作为生态方，共同构建农业商业生态，向生态方分享农业现代化的价值增值。

宁夏盐池滩羊的发展是一个典型的以品牌策划完善商业生态系统的案例。滩羊集团紧盯高端市场，紧抓国际国内重要会议，从政府和企业两端发力开拓市场，通过"以奖代补"鼓励产业链企业开发新产品，积极参加各类农产品展（博）览（销）会，加大营销力度，自主推介、开拓市场。盐池利用"G20峰会"、"金砖五国峰会"、"上合组织峰会"、大连"夏季达沃斯论坛"等国内国际大型会议会展活动，先后在杭州、深圳、上海、北京等大中城市举办"盐池滩羊"品牌宣传推介会，邀请大型餐饮企业、高端酒店、商超与商贸、物流等行业的商会、协会负责人参加。通过不断的品牌塑造，盐池滩羊肉区域品牌价值为70多亿元，品牌价值得到社会各界的充分认可，整个产业迈上新的发展台阶。这表明，品牌创意设计在生态农业六次产业化中发挥重要作用。

第三，拓展数字技术的应用空间，构建农业现代化的社会生态。 随着增强现实和虚拟现实等数字技术的发展，网络空间正在重构社会生态。在AI技术的支持下，"数字人"已经作为直播者开辟新赛道。乡村作为一个物理空间，因社交网络、购物平台、虚拟社区和场景，以及正在到来的元宇宙而发生深刻变化。乡村将是嵌入未来生活的重要场景，这种场景将是虚拟世界与现实世界的混合世界，它是一种新的社会生态。乡村社会生态不仅涉及人与自然的关系，也为乡村教育、医疗、养老、生物多样性保护以及粮食安全和气候变化等诸多问题的解决提供非常广阔的空间。其发展程度，一方面受数字技术进步的影响，另一方面受公共政策引导的影响。虽然目前基于农业现代化的社会生态还处于初级阶段，但可以预期将来会对乡村产生深刻影响。在农业强国战略下，为了实现农民农村共同富裕，我们需要提早部署基于农业现代化的社会生态。

（二）生态农业六次产业化

生态农业六次产业化，本质上是发展未来农业或健康农业，为人们的生命健康提供生态产品和服务。健康农业涉及两个方面：一是食品健康营养，解决人的健康问题；二是生态绿色，涉及人类的可持续发展。这与我们前面谈到的农业的自然生态、商业生态和社会生态密不可分。生态农业六次产业化，首先强调的是"生态农业"，即我国农业现代化要遵循农业的自然生态规律，走绿色发展道路。同时，在数字文明新时代，我国农业现代化要从数字经济的商业生态和社会生态中找到新的路径。也就是说，不仅要走绿色发展道路，还要构建农业现代化的商业生态和社会生态。否则，如何实现农民增收？

在气候变化的背景下，人类可持续发展面临严峻挑战，农业也不例外。2020 年 9 月 22 日，国家主席习近平在第七十五届联合国大会一般性辩论上郑重宣布，"中国将提高国家自主贡献力度，采取更加有力的政策和措施，二氧化碳排放力争于 2030 年前达到峰值，努力争取 2060 年前实现碳中和"。"碳达峰""碳中和"目标的承诺，要求我们必须深入贯彻生态文明理念，走绿色发展道路。在生态文明建设的理念指引下，我国高度重视涉农产业融合发展，有机农业、现代食品加工基地、现代农业产业园、绿色生态农庄、乡村文旅等在各地茁壮成长，农产品生产流通环节日臻完善，三产融合发展的产业链渐现雏形，并且呈现"星星之火"化成"燎原"之势。

从健康农业的角度来看，还需处理好人与社会、人与自然的关系。人的健康，不仅包括躯体健康、心理健康，还包括社会功能健康和人与自然的关系健康。在机器人、人工智能快速发展的数字经济时代，许多体力劳动甚至一般性的智力劳动都会被机器人、人工智能替代，特别是 ChatGPT 具有势不可当的态势。将来许多服务会被 ChatGPT 取代。这要求重新建构人与社会之间的关系。农民也面临同样的问题。此外，人与自然的关系是现代农业的另一关键所在。新冠疫情的发生有可能是由人与自然的关系被破坏所致。地球平均温度的上升，带来极端天气的增加，不仅吸引了科学家的关注，也切实关系到每个人的生存。

生态农业六次产业化就是遵循农业的自然规律，运用数字经济理论与数字技术，构建以用户终身体验价值为导向的商业生态系统，并且在此基础上逐步构建城乡融合的社会生态系统。这就要求，农业现代化走数字融合之路，充分利用生产数据的产业即第四产业的优势实现农村三产融合，创造新业态；除此以外，还要充分利用文化创意、智慧因子要素对农村产业甚至城乡融合产业进行创意化设计，即开辟第五产业。在第四产业、第五产业对农村三产进行融合的条件下，培育中国的未来农业。这就是我提出的生态农业六次产业化的基本概念框架。

（三）生态农业六次产业化理论逻辑

我们从四个方面简要说明生态农业六次产业化的理论逻辑，以后再专门设一章讨论生态农业六次产业化专项行动，为人们深入理解生态农业六次产业化提供理论和实践参考。

第一，生态农业六次产业化是数字文明时代的农业现代化。它不同于工业文明时代的农业现代化。工业化思维具有明确的分工与竞争，以产品为中心。那时，农业作为第一产业，处于产业链的最上游，为食品工业、化学工业、纺织工业等提供原材料。因此，农民在整个产业链中分享到的利益最少。正是在这种背景下，日本才提出把工业和服务业引入农村，增加农业产值，解决农村衰落的问题。生态农业六次产业化，把农民、农村和农业看作整个商业生态中的生态方，以设计用户终身体验价值为中心。生态方主要进行融合与共享。所谓融合就是融入整个生态系统中，所谓共享就是共享融合商业生态系统中的价值。因此，从经济学理论来看，现在已经发生了不同于工业经济的变革。如果说1900年有了新式拖拉机，农业经历了第一次革命，由机械工业带来农业生产率的大幅提升，美国、英国、法国都得益于第一次革命；之后化肥、农药、保鲜技术的发展，特别是现代生物技术引入农业，农业经历了第二次革命。现在，伴随着数字文明时代的到来，农业面临第三次革命。

第二，生态农业六次产业化以用户终身体验价值为中心。用户终身体验价值体现了以人为本的发展思想，以用户终身体验价值为中心，意味着这种体验不是一次性体验，农业除了提供产品之外，还提供文旅休闲、乡村空间和自然风光体验以及农业文明传承教育等服务。这要根据客户的需要进行系统设计。在不断的体验中，农业带来多次交易，农户可以获得多次收益。李子柒以农村生活为题材的流媒体创作以及内容营销，实质上是经过系统性创意设计的一种基于乡村生活的新服务。这种内容服务的核心是对用户体验价值的感知。李子柒的美食视频，包括农村自然生态，农产品的种植、采摘，美食加工等原生态的文化创意，以及有关川菜的乡村做法。她为远离自然环境的现代都市人带来一种人与自然、人与社会的亲切感，一种难以返回的乡愁，也为由创意驱动的乡村振兴——生态农业六次产业化提供了典型案例。

第三，生态农业六次产业化需要生态合约设计。生态合约设计不同于工业经济的供应链上下游采购合同，采购合同明确标的、产品的质量要求，通过产品标准化信息降低交易成本。生态合约设计的前提不是一次性交易，要围绕用户体验价值进行长期可持续发展设计，利益是共生的，其关键是形成共生生态环境、共生组织模式和共生行为模式。这三点非常重要，一个生态农业六次产业化系统包括：共生生态环境、共生组织模式和共生行为模式。同样，对于李子柒自2021年7月以来的停播，问题出在了生态合约的破裂上，生态系统中的共生生态环境、共生组织模式和共享利益受到了破坏。生态合约设计是数字化时代的新商业模式，它需要专业培训和系统设计，以构筑"三个共生"，保证商业生态系统的可持续发展。生态合约设计的关键是要找到生态方，不是所有事情都要从头做起。

第四，生态农业六次产业化涉及链群模式的产业化组织。刚才我们讲构筑"三个共生"，其中之一涉及共生组织，我们称这种组织为"链群模式的产业化组织"。工业经济时代以产品和服务为核心，它的组织方式为股权结构。因此，很多企业家的想法是实现一股独大，赢者通吃，小股东只是用来点缀公司股权结构而已，强烈的工业色彩往往使公司走向垄断。但是生态经济不强调股权结构，强调的是链群结构。什么是链群结构？因为生态农业六次产业化的核心是用户终身体验价值，所以谁为用户价值做出贡献，我们就称谁为生态方。生态方的链接是通过数字化条件下的链群，用链群合约或者链群共同体实现的。所以这个合约在区块链与第三代互联网条件下是完全可以执行的，其执行能力比工业化时代的股权结构的执行能力更有效、更牢固。正是有了区块链思维和区块链技术支持，链群模式的产业化组织才能降低信息获得的交易成本，才能形成相对稳定的组织结构，从而可以共生、共享。

案例解析：生态农业六次产业化如何破解"三农"问题

六次产业理论的创造者张来武教授在宁夏回族自治区人民政府工作十年，当时的宁夏山大沟深、干旱少雨、生态脆弱、交通不便，信息闭塞，科技落后。宁夏西海固更是在1972年被世界粮食计划署称为最不适宜人类生存的地区之一，是"农业禁区"。

在这样一个生态环境下，宁夏之所以能建立起与世界知名葡萄酒产区媲美的酿酒葡萄产地，打造出"蓝色奇迹"，是因为它一直向生态农业六次产业化探索实践。尽管现在尚未形成理想的数字文明时代的生态农业六次产业化模式，但是它已经具备这样的案例特征。接下来，我将从生态、数据和科技三个方面说明宁夏酿酒葡萄产业如何正在迈向生态农业六次产业化发展模式。

首先，宁夏的自然条件决定其必须进行绿色发展转型，以调整人与自然的关系。宁夏水资源严重缺乏，一些地方是废弃的采矿区，不可能走美国式的农业现代化道路。宁夏的农业、工业发展，必须采用节水模式，这是由自然资源禀赋所决定的，宁夏贺兰山东麓废弃矿区进行生态改造，人工建造了上万亩葡萄园。如今，贺兰山东麓酿酒葡萄种植面积达到 58 万亩，这里是中国最大的酿酒葡萄集中连片产区，实现了山水林田湖草沙综合治理，使 35 万亩荒滩变绿洲，成片的葡萄园在贺兰山东麓形成了一条绿色生态屏障。这既有政府的顶层设计，也有东西部协作机制下来自福建省的企业家的投入和创新，更有当地老百姓的辛苦劳作。

其次，宁夏必须进行信息化、数字化转型，以降低生产成本和交易成本。作为全国的农村信息化建设试点地区，2008 年，宁夏率先在全区开启新型农民信息化培训工程，主要目的是培养一批掌握信息技术的新型农民，加快全区新农村信息化步伐。宁夏当时的农村信息化采取了"强势领导、多方推进，创新共赢、多网融合，平台上移、服务下延，整合资源、个性服务、多元投资、长效机制"的做法。农村信息化首先在中卫市的硒砂瓜、枸杞产业基地试点。在宁夏全区的 2362 个行政村，每个村建立一个信息服务站，再把这些信息服务站互联互通，形成一个整体。当时构建了两个平台：一个是 IPTV 平台，另一个是电子商务专业平台。每个平台背后有大量的数据工作，没有这些工作，平台就没有内容。一个中心平台（IPTV 平台）、一个专业平台（电子商务专业平台），加上网络终端形成了一个农村信息化服务平台大框架。它的基本功能是帮助农民在互联网上经营，包括三个方面：一是，对于生产中遇到的技术问题可以通过互联网、呼叫中心，找到能够解决问题的专家和办法；二是，互联网可以帮助销售农产品，农民可以连接大市场，还能找到要买的东西；三是，发展文化共享工程。这就构成了宁夏农村信息化的互联网经营、互联网文化和互联网培训三大功能，我们叫"三网合一"，当时我们提出，未来要"一网打天下"，涉及"三农"的所有互联网服务都要并在这个网中。所有信息服务站要一站多用，实现服务下延。在建设上采取整合共建的思路，包括信息资源整合、平台资源整合、网络资源整合、组织资源整合、资金资源整合、社会资源整合，通过全方位的资源整合，建设一个广泛的、及时更新的、有效益的、有价值的数据库。事实上，宁夏农村信息化的先行先试，为之后宁夏硒砂瓜产业、枸杞产业、滩羊产业、酿酒葡萄产业的发展奠定了数据新要素基础。

最后，宁夏农村产业的发展充分利用了科技要素。作为与农民"风险共担，利益共享"的创新创业模式，科技特派员制度弥补了政府农业技术推广部门的服务能力的不足。科技特派员利用自己掌握的技术，与农民、合作社等农业经营主体建立了商业生态，这个生态的核心就是利用各自的优势资源，进行资源整合，开辟新的商业模式，把价值增值与农民分享。它既不同于政府科技推广部门的自上而下的单方向的公共服务提供模式，也不同于农机制造商、化肥厂家与农民的一次性买卖交易市场化模式，采用一种合作与共享的理念。这也体现了生态农业六次产业化的思想。农村科技特派员成为"科技下乡、服务下沉、合作经营、利益分成"的生态方。

以上比较抽象化地对生态农业六次产业化的生态、数据和科技三个方面进行了说明。现在我们结合宁夏酿酒葡萄产业的发展进一步谈谈如何落地。

第一，刚才我们说从生态、数据和科技三个方面说明生态农业六次产业化的核心要素，但是，宁夏酿酒葡萄产业的发展并不排斥工业化带来的技术进步。宁夏各大葡萄酒酒庄的生产厂家，充分利用现代生物技术和工业技术的成果，把先进的发酵技术、法国先进的酿酒工艺融入产业链中。此外，宁夏葡萄酒酒庄在参观路线、展示内容、休闲娱乐等方面都做了精心的设计。这种设计实质上就是瞄准前来旅游观光的用户的体验价值，以体验价值为中心，或者说产品价值设计充分考虑用户的体验价值，贯彻生态农业六次产业化的"以人为中心"的思想。

第二，走产业融合发展的道路。以贺兰山东麓葡萄连片种植区为代表的第一产业，以由先进酿酒工艺支撑的现代化工业企业为代表的第二产业，以葡萄酒精品旅游线路为实施路径，串接沿线旅游景点、酒庄、精品民宿，对接乡村振兴战略构筑新型服务业，形成"葡萄种植＋酿酒生产＋文化旅游＋康养"等多产业融合发展态势，使贺兰山东麓产业发展面貌焕然一新。这与只把旅游业作为附加环节的旧酒庄经营理念完全不同。

第三，宁夏酿酒葡萄产业构筑了一个庞大的商业生态系统。从这个新的商业生态系统来看，它包括若干生态方：在种植环节，有种植大户、合作社、葡萄基地；在生产环节，有先进的葡萄酒酿造工艺和设备工业企业；在营销环节，有各种各样进行创意设计的酒庄，引入了酒庄文化。其结果是形成了以成片的葡萄种植为代表的果园文化，以葡萄酒酿造工艺、设备和酒器为象征的葡萄酒酿造工业文化体系，以葡萄酒品鉴文化、酒俗酒礼为依托的侍酒文化体系，以及丝路风情、区域旅游等文旅体系。近年来，在数字经济的推动下，网络营销者、直播等流媒体也作为新的生态方进入宁夏酿酒葡萄产业。

贺兰神国际酒庄，已在戈壁荒滩上种植了3000亩酿酒葡萄、9000亩林木，并先后对6000亩废弃矿区进行生态修复。宁夏酿酒葡萄产业首先走的是一条自然生态路径，"不与人争粮、不与粮争地、水资源高效利用"是宁夏酿酒葡萄产业的主要特征之一。在此基础上，构建了商业生态，并逐步构建社会生态。虽然我们不能说宁夏酿酒葡萄产业已经实现生态农业六次产业化，特别是在新要素、新模式和新主流方面还有很多文章可做，在用户终身体验价值设计上也有很多文章可做，但它已经接近我们所说的生态农业六次产业化。

问题3：何为未来农业？

未来农业是可持续发展的农业。过去，发达国家的农业现代化大量消耗石化能源，为提高农业生产率提供源源不断的机械动力和化学肥料、除草剂、保鲜剂等。但今天，中国农业除了要确保粮食安全以外，还有一个最重要的约束条件，那就是必须走绿色发展的道路，采用生态农业模式。这就要求，中国未来农业商业模式基于"碳中和"形成。在实现"碳中和"的过程中，通过生物技术进步，发现新的商业模式。未来很多地方不适合种粮食，但是适合进行基于"碳吸收"的种植。通过把生物科技和数字科技结合起来，不仅能解决"碳吸收"问题，还能把"碳指标"的数字平台建立起来。通过数字化的生态农业，不仅能把"碳指标"测算出来，还能把"碳指标"做成交易产品和具有高附加值的产品，生态农业可以形成新的产业模式、商业模式，在数字技术的支持下，生态资产可以转化为农民的资产，从而实现生态价值转换。

首先，未来农业是健康农业。这一点非常重要，我们需要从人的躯体健康、心理健康、社会健康和生态健康等多个维度评价农业的健康功能。也就是说，相比过去农业以保障食物安全为主，转向更加突出强调农业的多功能性。从育种、种植、管理、加工、仓储、物流直到食品走上餐桌，生态系统中的任何一个节点都需要贯彻绿色发展理念，采取生态环境友好型技术。这样的农业生产经营活动充分考虑了人与自然和谐共生的关系，在生态系统中考虑农业的发展。此外，即使人类社会从工业文明时代进入数字文明新时代，也不可能抛弃农耕文明。尤其对于中国人来说，它是炎黄以来传承下来的一种文明，是人类文明之一。不能说农业产值占 GDP 的比重下降，农业就业人口减少，就弱化农业文明的重要性。从这层含义来讲，我想强调的是农业还具有社会功能。

其次，未来农业是数智农业。未来农业基于先进通信技术、人工智能、生物技术等前沿技术与农业的深度融合而发展。以农业的"芯片"种子为例，在生物技术与人工智能的交叉应用下，可以选育耐盐碱的品种，在此基础上，中国大面积的盐碱地可能转化为大面积良田。这是完全不同的技术路径，过去我们主要对盐碱地进行改造，积累了比较丰富的经验，但投资巨大，很难持续。将来如果我们用生物技术与人工智能在育种上做出新文章，就将开辟盐碱农业蓝海。现在智能化温室管理、农产品物流派送、预制菜派送已经发展到可以提供个性化、定制化服务。以后，人工智能技术的进一步发展可以做到根据客户需求定制营养菜单。这样的农业使得人类掌握更加健康长寿的生活模式。

人类天才的最伟大发现，便是自然秩序结构和心灵结构之间完美的契合。未来经济和未来产业模式的契合将形成未来的生态产业。总之，人类社会对气候变化和可持续发展的关注，需要走生态农业现代化道路，而生态农业的发展需要六次产业化，六次产业化的关键是要注重数字化转型。在农业的数字化转型中，农业生态产品不仅要满足人们的物质需求，还要满足人们的情感需求、精神需求；生态农业六次产业化不仅要充分地利用工业化时代的文明，而且，更重要的是，在数字化时代，创造新的文明、新的产业模式。未来农业需要进行生态化、数字化设计，构建农业的自然生态、商业生态和社会生态，通过对用户终身体验价值以及链群产业组织模式的设计，从分工与竞争走向融合与共享。数字文明时代为我国迈向农业现代化提供了新机遇，也为我们解决城乡二元结构问题提供了新机遇。因此，可以说，生态农业六次产业化就是在打造未来农业。未来农业是与现代工业共生的新型产业！

第三章　如何培育生态农业六次产业化专项

问题 1：为什么要提出生态农业六次产业化专项？

从 2016 年在西北农林科技大学和复旦大学分别创建六次产业研究院以来，2018 年，我在人民出版社出版了第一本六次产业理论著作——《六次产业理论与创新驱动发展》。著作出版后受到读者的广泛关注，许多企业家，包括农业企业家，特别关心如何操作六次产业。2016~2018 年，从成立"六产两院"这样的理论机构到标志性理论著作的出版，我们开创了六次产业理论，构建了一个推动生态农业六次产业化发展的理论体系。在这个理论框架下，我们提出生态农业六次产业化的关键在于数字化，在于第四产业；生态农业六次产业化的顶级策划设计属于文化创意范畴，属于第五产业。那么，由谁来设计？对此，我们也做了一些开创性工作，包括创办了一个社会组织，即由杨凌示范区科技局作为主管部门的民办非企业单位——六次产业创新中心。基于此，我们一方面具有了理论准备，另一方面通过民办非企业单位可以从事一些社会策划工作。

为什么在这个阶段，我们要提出生态农业六次产业化专项？这涉及三个问题。

第一个问题，生态农业六次产业化的中国特色体现在哪里？生态农业六次产业化与中国的农村科技特派员制度密切相关。前面我们说，中国的农村科技特派员制度和日本的农业六次产业化是六次产业理论的两个实践来源，而数字经济和创意设计特别是人工智能在创意设计领域的深度介入，为六次产业理论提供了新的创立条件。正是基于中国农村科技特派员制度20多年来的成功实践，我们与中国软科学研究会科技特派员工作委员会共同设计了一个生态农业六次产业化专项。这个专项的主要目的是应用六次产业理论策划生态农业发展模式，即生态农业六次产业化。生态农业六次产业理论与传统生态农业理论并不相同，它不仅要求农业的发展遵循自然生态，还需构建数字文明时代的商业生态和社会生态。其中，商业生态对应第四产业，即数据产业；社会生态对应第五产业，即来自新时代的人文、文化创意甚至科学前沿的创意产业。如果只将其理解成原有的自然生态，其就成为传统的农业工业化，那么很多有关科学与人文的附加值就跟农业无关，也就无法形成高附加值的有良性循环的健康农业。

第二个问题，形成这样的生态农业六次产业化，需要具备怎样的战略举措与抓手？解决该问题的关键在于整个农业的数字化转型。没有数据产业，也就没有六次产业化，没有数字技术平台，就很难形成六次产业化，那么生态农业六次产业化就无法做到，也无法操作形成新的业态和实现价值增值。数据产业与生态农业之间建立联系，需要进行若干设计。这个我们稍后再谈。

第三个问题，这一次专项由谁来进行孵化？顶级的策划设计对六次产业理论来说是最重要的，那么谁来策划？西北农林科技大学六次产业研究院和复旦大学六次产业研究院是六次产业研究的发源地。生态农业六次产业化在操作模式上有一个重大创新——"六产两院"和民办非企业单位联合策划了一个专项——生态农业六次产业化专项。我们准备跟中国软科学研究会科技特派员工作委员会进行政社产学研融合带动。依托这些组织、研究机构把它推广为全国的专项行动，由此成为乡村振兴、产业振兴的重要战略举措。这不仅可以探索解决中国千年来存在的城乡二元结构问题，还可以引领未来农业。将来，更多掌握了六次产业理论的智库、商业策划机构可以加入生态农业六次产业化设计，共同推动中国式农业现代化发展。

问题 2：什么是生态农业六次产业化专项？

我国农业产业化始终落后于工业化，当前我国的农业全要素生产率约为60%，与美国、荷兰等发达国家相比，还有不小的差距，因此我国第一产业的兴旺程度较低。如何壮大第一产业，如何持续增加农民收入，如何不断改善农村环境？这是一直困扰我们的难题。中央提出实现三产融合发展，并且出台了不少政策支持农村产业融合发展，取得了不少成效。三产融合发展的理念其实来源于六次产业理论。但是，大家对于农业六次产业理论与实践的认识都很模糊，对三产融合的理解也很浅。一方面，大家主要把"接二连三"理解为产业融合；另一方面，很多实践打着六次产业化的名义却做的是三产融合的工作。但这些都不是我们所说的六次产业化，原因就在于缺乏理论指导。

新华社对复旦大学六次产业研究院做过采访，其将六次产业理论报告给中央，接着公开指出，在日本、韩国、德国，特别是中国，农业六次产业化以燎原之势在发展。采访中，我向其表示，日本是六次产业发展的代表国家，而中国创造了六次产业理论。那么，中国与日本的六次产业有何区别？在六次产业理论上，中国与日本各有三个方面的优势。

中国的优势有以下三个。第一，中国有六次产业理论。日本第六产业只是一个概念，它的理论是对三次产业条件下的农业经济学的突破，指的就是"接二连三"，把加工业和服务业吸引到农村，让农民分享第二、三产业的利益。但是，日本根本没有第四产业，也没有第五产业，何来的六次产业。第二，中国的数字化水平超过日本。中国有阿里巴巴、京东、腾讯、拼多多、抖音等互联网平台公司，这些平台公司都参与到了农产品营销之中，在数字化的第四产业方面，日本远不及中国。第三，中国有农村科技特派员制度。后文中有一章专门讲中国的农村科技特派员制度。农村科技特派员制度是由掌握一定技术的企业、专业技术人员到农村，以"风险共担，利益共享"的经营模式与农民共同创业。农村科技特派员制度是中国六次产业理论的实践来源之一，利用城市企业家的力量与农民合作进行全产业链操作。

日本的三个优势如下。第一，机械化。日本的工业化、机械化程度比中国高，或者说走在前面，特别是小微农机具有世界一流水平，设施农业也相当先进。第二，农协的文明程度。它可以有效地把农民组织起来，提供统一的生产资料、统一的农产品，以及为农户提供信贷、保险等金融服务。日本农协有利于六次产业化发展，有利于推进三产融合发展。农协的优势带来了什么？其带来惠及农民、日本六次产业化的发展。在利益分配上，即使没有六次产业，没有第四、五产业，在三次产业中，其也能实现农民分享第二、三产业的利益。第三，日本六次产业化的实践的普及程度很高，2008年，日本已经针对其进行立法。从21世纪开始，这种产业化便遍及日本很多农村。

对以上优势比较下来，可以看到最重要的六次产业理论始于中国。我们系统地提出并且对其进行深化。六次产业理论随着数字经济的发展而不断深化。就像脱农化的时候工业化理论是新理论，六次产业理论是工业化以后的数字化时代的新理论。正是基于新华社的此次报道，我们觉得有必要推出生态农业六次产业化专项。第一，聚焦生态农业策划，既接促进产业兴旺的地气又符合可持续发展大势；第二，遵循时代要求发展和践行六次产业理论，历史时机不可延误。工业文明时代的经济学创新主要来自美国、英国、德国、法国等发达国家，而我们有可能在数字文明时代对经济学理论做出一点贡献。这便是生态农业六次产业化专项的价值。有日本六次产业化和中国农村科技特派员制度的成功实践，有中国在世界领先的第四产业，我们在第五产业领域开展创意设计，用创意设计驱动生态农业六次产业化落地，还是可行的。

问题3：生态农业六次产业化专项如何操作？

按照六次产业理论，第四产业便是将数据产业应用到生态农业上，形成数字化的农业商业生态；第五产业是智慧农业和文化创意农业，形成农业的人文社会生态；第六产业将生态农业变成一个社会共享的产业，从而获得融合产业的利益。以下，我们首先谈谈数据农业创新怎么做，也就是如何打造第四产业，如何推动农业和第四产业融合？

（一）数据农业创新怎么做

现阶段，国家统计局已经接受我们提出的六次产业理论的两大观点：第一个观点，数据是关键的生产要素；第二个观点，继农业经济、工业经济之后，数字经济是主要的经济形态。国家统计局发布的《数字经济及其核心产业统计分类（2021）》明确指出，数字经济是指以数据资源为关键生产要素、以现代信息网络为重要载体、以信息通信技术的有效使用为效率提升和经济结构优化的重要推动力的一系列经济活动。并且将数字经济产业范围确定为01"数字产品制造业"、02"数字产品服务业"、03"数字技术应用业"、04"数字要素驱动业"、05"数字化效率提升业"五大类。国家实施"数字中国战略"，抢占数字经济先机，分享数字经济红利。基于这个原因，我们有理由认为，数据产业已经可以被成熟地应用。这样的话，数据产业可以被应用到生态农业中，变成农业的第四产业来运作。

第一，把数据产业应用到生态农业中。虽然第四产业不分农业、非农业，但它可以优先服务于农业。在六次产业理论中，第四产业被称为"互联网⊕"，现在逐渐走向重视数据，也叫作数据产业。从平台经济开始走向重视数据以来，数据不只是数字，数字要实现生产要素化，数据要采集、要处理，对它的处理包括确权、定价、交易、应用等一系列生产工序。中国有很多平台都在尝试这样做。首先依据的是互联网的平台经济，没有平台，便无法采集、沉淀、应用数据，这就是数据产业的形态。而数据产业是通过四个专业（产业）模块发挥作用。第一个模块是算力成本，智慧农业的发展需要考虑谁来提供算力，成本几何；第二个模块是软件快速迭代能力；第三个模块是知识沉淀、数据沉淀；第四个模块是社会网络协同。数据产业的四个模块跟工业化的情况完全不同，在工业化背景下，企业就是边界，第四产业要求四个模块具备社会协同能力。社会协同是发展第四产业的基础，社会协同才能使得数据共享的成分合理。只要把第四产业包括的四个模块中的任何一个模块做好，就有建立生态的余地。一个产业做好了，别的产业就会有求于你，你就能带动第一、二、三产业发展，就能找到很多的商业合作者。

第二，关注生态农业要解决的问题。六次产业理论认为，最重要的是生态农业创新链一定要实现全流程整合，绝不要试图参与供应链上的每一个节点，那是工业化思维，强调的是分工与竞争。在数字经济时代，供应链是必需的，但更重要的是进行创新链的全流程整合，进行整合设计。在数字化时代，生态农业若想有商业生态和社会生态，就需要新的生态要素——数据。因此，不能单打独斗、为所欲为，要讲究合作与共享，构建共生生态。一定要设计好、衔接好，鼓励生态系统中的各个主体达成合作共识，实现共享和共赢合作。在整合全流程中，要先解决市场附加值和销售能力的问题，而不是倒过来。现在我们的思维多数是"我有什么技术、做什么事"，那么在这里要找到六次产业化思维，找到附加值来源。比如，李子柒的附加值的来源是棉被的故事，而不是一床棉被，这个故事满足了人们的精神需求，而不是满足了人们盖棉被的物质需求。新的高附加值需求的销售方式是自媒体，不是电商，更不是那些成本巨高的传统销售网络。自媒体销售需要进行一整套创意设计，这就要求第五产业与第四产业紧密相连。策划创意要符合规律，内容要打动人心，让人们愿意付出高附加值。此外，在新时代，销售领域更重要的是反推机制，反推机制首先来自客户的体验价值，绝不是生产者自己的体验，更不是动不动花钱搞一个巨大的销售团队，先生产产品，再去推销。工业化时代的营销模式已经过去了，有销售网络固然是重要的，但是并不需要更多的企业来建立销售网络，采用这种自媒体销售模式往往会取得惊人的成功。新东方董宇辉卖农产品，也具有相同的道理，人们从他的讲解中体验到了新的价值，而这个价值不是来自农产品本身。它来自新东方的文化创意价值，来自董宇辉个人呈现和表达的文化精神价值。

第三，要解决全产业链不衔接的问题。不衔接的地方在哪里？往往在第四产业，那些互联网平台企业跟农民连接不起来，跟供应链的初端、原始端也连接不起来。同时，金融也连接不起来。对于供应链金融，为什么就连银行也做不下去？问题就出现在供应链中仓储数据的真实性方面。比如，实际上没有货时，企业却声称有货，在玩概念，先把银行的钱拿去，在市场需要货的时候往往没有货，即使有货也不是原来的货。为什么与农民签订的产品合约不稳定？因为即使你与农民签订了采购合同，今年农民把产品卖给你了，明年也可能不卖给你。今年给你这个价，明年给你那个价。那么在操作中怎么处理呢？从理论上说，有两个渠道：一个是把农民组织起来，如日本农协；另一个是建立农业物联网，让数据真实可信，降低交易成本。把农民组织起来后，日本农协的优势便展现出来。中国的农民组织化程度低，会出现各种不稳定因素，这样的话，全产业链整体设计体系便构建不起来。从这个角度说，我们调研了很多供应链金融案例，发现其都在与农民连接的环节出现了问题，这就是所谓当年很多互联网企业包括京东、拼多多下沉都失败的原因。按道理来讲，拼多多跟农民的联系很紧密，在农产品电商方面做了很多事，但仍然面临连接不起来的挑战。这是因为农民没有被组织起来，农业基地不可能跟互联网时代的这样一个平台天然相连。那么怎么办？这时农村科技特派员制度可以发挥组织农民的作用，农业物联网也可以发挥重要作用。华为正在积极地推行这件事，希望用传感器、智能化手段解决与大产地的连接问题。宁夏葡萄酒产业目前还没连接物联网，如果宁夏的酿酒葡萄种植采用物联网，葡萄酒六次产业就能做得更好。可以说，农业物联网跟第一产业数据下沉是密切相连的，要么把农民组织起来，要么构建物联网。或者说，二者都需要。

（二）第五产业如何形成

我国第四产业发展得很快，中国信息通信研究院发布的《中国数字经济发展研究报告（2023 年）》中的数据显示，我国数字经济总体规模已经超过 50 万亿元。我国拥有全球规模最大、技术领先的网络基础设施，算力基础设施达到世界领先水平。也就是说，我国正在分享第四产业红利。那么，进一步的价值增值空间就在第五产业。普遍实现生态农业六次产业化，需要有大量的适应数字化时代的创业者，特别是要有文化创意的创业者。这些创业者把农业的自然生态、农耕文明、乡土文化、民族文化等与数字技术结合起来，进行创意设计，为农业产业的价值增值找到更加广阔的空间。各位读者，希望你们未来可以成为创业者，就算是教授也可以创业，现在中央鼓励教授创业。做企业家更要创业，哪怕做农民，也要做数字化时代的职业农民，从而在农业生态六次产业化中为中国的乡村振兴尽一份力。这里我想突出强调的是，这个创意不是为了满足物质的需求，是为了满足人们的精神生活需求。对于元宇宙中的地产，我们在物质上享受不到，但是它卖得很贵，因为这一套东西是基于文化创意的创新产品。

农业农村部农村经济研究中心与尚浓智库主办印迹乡村创意设计大赛，印迹乡村创意设计大赛是印迹乡村文化工程的一项重要内容。该工程是落实中央关于实施乡村振兴战略的部署和要求，在农业农村部指导下开展的以乡愁情感为纽带，以文化活动为载体，动员社会力量助力乡村振兴建设的一项综合性工作，包括印迹乡村档案馆建设、印迹乡村之旅、印迹乡村文创等内容。第二届印迹乡村创意设计大赛的主题是"创意发掘多元价值 设计引领未来乡村"。通过创意设计挖掘、传承、创新优秀传统乡土文化，促进宜居宜业乡村建设和现代乡村产业提质增效，鼓励各类人才参与乡村振兴事业。这就是用六次产业理论的思想，通过大赛来推动乡村文化创意产业发展。在某种程度上，印迹乡村创意设计大赛采用政社产学研联合的方式推进。农业农村部农村经济研究中心作为国家乡村振兴的智库，指导大赛，保证其贯彻落实乡村振兴方针政策。在大赛进行中，专家学者、智库机构、创意设计团队、高校师生以及相关乡村等多元主体积极参与。大赛围绕建设农业强国的中心任务，突出中国乡村文化理念，推动现代设计理念与传统农耕文明深度融合，围绕村庄建设、乡村景观和公共设施，以及农产品包装等进行创意设计，为建设宜居宜业和美乡村、赋能乡村经济、促进乡村社会发展提供有力支撑。

这个时代为什么能形成第五产业，如果退回到工业化时代，退回到农业时代，那么有故事可讲却成不了产业。只有数字化时代能提供讲故事的基础，即第四产业能够提供数字化的这种产业模型。更重要的是，工业化以后，物质文明高度发达，生活主流开始发生变化，人们以对梦想、情感等精神生活的追求为主流。与上一代人的想法不一样，这个时代的人追求的是自由、情感、梦想、理想。你不得不承认，人类生活主流已经悄悄地发生变迁。变迁的附加值是生态农业的附加值来源。为什么元宇宙中的很多产业是具有高附加值的，就是因为它满足了人们的精神需求。如今，一方面，在需求侧，社会大众的精神文化需求增多；另一方面，供给侧发生了快速变革。进入新媒体时代，人们的交流主要以新媒体为媒介，它催生了文化传播方式的变革。新媒体的发展推动数字文化创意产业发展，使得一些优秀传统文化，如农耕文化、乡土文化可以借助新媒体平台快速传播。此外，数字文化创意产业中的数码娱乐、虚拟生态空间服务，丰富了网络文化。艺术设计领域也迎来了新的变革，数字艺术产品可以进行数字确权、数字交易，网上展览。这些需求与供给的共同变革，使得第五产业可以服务于乡村振兴。

在当今世界上，数字虚拟产品满足了人们的精神生活需求，伴随着生活主流发生变迁，供给与需求匹配，最终便会形成第五产业。加上印迹乡村创意设计大赛这样的政社产学研联合的方式推动，相信在不久的将来，第五产业一定会成为中国特色乡村振兴的一个重要组成部分。

问题 4：如何创新驱动生态农业六次产业化？

（一）关于科学的认知

要谈创新驱动生态农业六次产业化，必须明白什么是科学。近代以来，我们对科学的认识出现了一些误解，有的是一知半解的。什么是科学？我们先谈谈欧拉"神的公式"。

"神的公式"是什么？就是欧拉通过函数向人们展示"$1+2+3+\cdots\cdots=-1/12$"。从表现上看，这个公式是不合理的，一加二加三加到无穷，一直加下去，有点数学常识的人肯定说等于无穷大，为什么一直往下加？而且都是正数，一直加下去，那不就是无穷？大多数人认可这个结论。但是让大家吃惊的是，欧拉给的结论是 –1/12。欧拉是人类历史上的四大数学家之首，他给的答案是 –1/12，所有人都惊呆了，只能说这是"神的公式"。后来拉马努金进行了初等证明，这个证明是可以看得懂的，正确的答案是 –1/12。后来还有人用黎曼函数证明，还是这个答案。这叫科学。

我用"神的公式"告诉大家什么是科学。科学的本质是什么？它真正的发展动力是什么？既然是基于科学的创新，它的根本目的是什么？"神的公式"的生成与物质、技术毫无关系。科学的发展的真正动力是人的生存方式。所以刚才用"神的公式"这个例子告诉人们我们研究它干什么。欧拉用它创造了一系列奇迹，虽然看起来没用，但这才是真正的科学。

科学的前沿的很多东西是从这里产生的，让人惊讶的是，原来科学居然是人的世界。许多人之前理解科学是技术的事情，科学是物的东西，其实不是的，科学是为了人的生存方式而出现的。基于此时对科学的理解，还可以再问下去：大家知道科学的起源吗？科学仅仅源于古希腊，除了古希腊以外，再无科学。在19世纪之前，科学跟技术处于两个轨道，互不来往。仅在近代，19世纪之后，科学技术化成为这一个阶段的特点。在近代，中国学习西方的科学。那西方的科学本质是什么？用爱因斯坦的一句话来说，西方科学的发展以两个伟大的成就为基础：希腊哲学家发明形式逻辑体系（在欧几里得几何中），以及（在文艺复兴时期）发现通过系统的实验可能找出因果关系。逻辑体系主要反映在欧几里得几何中，它完全是形式识别，是哲学家的产物，跟技术一点关系都没有，它有非常浓重的人文色彩。

对于这样两大成就的基础，六次产业理论认为，在数字化时代，科学产生了一个新的基础——人工智能。人工智能可以不研究因果关系，而研究关联关系。人工智能带来了一个新体系，一个新的科学范式，我认为这是科研的新方式。搞科研的功利性不要太重，要渴望争议、渴望自由、充满好奇心并乐此不疲，就像欧拉一样，仿佛为写出"神的公式"而生。让人们感到疯狂，但这就是科学。

现在焦点回到我们国家。19世纪以来，我国面临民族危机，学习西方的科学以救亡图存。之后我们由于落后而不断地追赶，恰好人类的科学发展进入一个技术化、分割化、职业化、力量化的阶段。这种巧合与我国国情结合，使国人对科学的理解有误，只知道做技术，不知道理解科学。由于理解科学被耽误了，社会对人文科学精神感到陌生。大家更加注重技术而不重视科学。我们的教育，特别是工科教育，只知道解题、做实验，对科学的历史背景、哲学前提和社会学逻辑都不太在意。我们整个社会对科学出现了误解，所以社会走偏了，科学走偏了，教育走偏了。西方科学在技术化、职业化、力量化阶段的发展促成了这样的现状，特别在军事和工业领域。但是数字化时代为我们提供了新的历史机遇，需要我们重新摆正对科学的理解，利用我们的智慧适应这个时代。

技术化、职业化的力量来源于创新的加速，信息化也同创新有关。信息化来源于工业化的加速，来源于创新的加速，显示出科学的产业威力、军事威力、技术威力。但是它延伸的创新理论是落后的。在数字化时代，科学知识可以不通过技术直接进入生产一线，直接应用于生产。所以，我不断强调"科学－技术－市场应用"三螺旋创新要特别注意科学可以直接产生服务，而不用经过技术转化。其实 AlphaGo 就是这样，它把人们对围棋的理解直接带到数据里面，三天"走完"人类千年的围棋文明史。以 AlphaGo 为代表的人工智能产品，通过关联研究直接进行操作，形成竞争力，成为赢家。基于科学的创新要求首先了解什么是科学，为什么要把科学跟技术作为两个不同的螺旋，但是它不排除技术，有些技术来源于科学发现。在 19 世纪以前，技术方面的发明基本上跟科学没有关系，近代以来，两者才相互关联起来。因此，现在科学与数据关联，有时候不需要通过技术，依靠的是知识能力和创意能力。随着 AI 技术的不断发展，科学可以直接创新服务方式。我们不仅要发展和依靠技术，还要繁荣科学，这就是我强调的重点。

（二）三螺旋条件下的创新

在科学、技术和市场应用三螺旋条件下，首先要知道基于科学的创新带来的是什么，尤其是在数字化时代，把基于科学创新以满足人们的情感共享生活作为主流是完全说得通的。为了生产工业化的物质产品，有时候可能会遇到一些工艺上的障碍，然而，对于在元宇宙中的生产经营，只要你基于科学知识发现事情可以做到，就可以立即实现，无须技术。这并不是说技术无用，我更想强调科学可以直接转化为未来服务。理解这一点非常重要。我对元宇宙持欢迎的态度。但是我觉得从六次产业理论的角度看元宇宙，就会发现现在有些热门的观点是有问题的。这些炒作元宇宙概念的人是积极的，他们认为在元宇宙虚拟市场中不需要技术，没有工业化的拖累，它在数字世界里能够翱翔，能够创新，能够不断地带来商机和丰富的科学内容，不断带来新的生活方式和新的社会组织方式。元宇宙是由美国作家尼尔·斯蒂芬森（Neal Stephenson）写的一部科幻小说《雪崩》提出来的，市场上热炒的元宇宙只是用了一个概念，经过炒作，当它传到中国时就变成了"《圣经》"。不能否认它有创新价值，但这样理解元宇宙是不完整的。

　　元宇宙把世界分解为与物质世界平行的宇宙，这是不必要的。我们怎么看元宇宙？六次产业理论认为，不同的世界、不同的时代，都是人类的统一宇宙。只不过元宇宙是数字世界里的时代。在这个时代，不仅有元宇宙的数字世界，还有物质世界、精神世界。世界从来没有被分裂，它只是在科学的领域里被人为分裂。所以，从这个角度来说，我们认为六次产业已经深入数字化时代了，何须再无能为力地去把它分成两个平行世界。这证明元宇宙的概念并不是什么了不起的固化的概念。

科学就是让人异想天开。异想天开给人类带来精彩绝伦的生活方式，迎接它，人就获得新生，活得精彩，脱离苦海，为什么不迎接呢？"神的公式"都能创造，自由的生活为什么不能迎接呢？有了这样一个三螺旋理论，新的科学发现就能直接进入市场，没有专利也不要苦恼。没有系统的商业知识，也照样可以在元宇宙中经营。在这样一个世界，当有很多精彩的东西跟我们所处的工业化社会衔接的时候，与元宇宙完全脱离物质世界不同，我们认为要融合物质和精神两个世界。那么，有很多东西既会看到工业化的力量，又能看到数字化的前景。

从这个角度来说，实现生态农业六次产业化最需要的就是生物技术和安全技术。我举一个例子——协生农场进行说明。传统的农业方法（如喷洒农药、使用化肥、投入人工与机械）的目的就是让产量高一些，质量好一些，能把产品卖个好价格。但是，协生农场则不同，通过将生物技术和数字技术结合起来，能够创造一种新的农业方法。协生农场利用多种植物的特性，通过进行高低度不同植物的混种，形成最优化的自然生长环境，让植物形成最优生态环境。人们经常说野生的更值钱，那么野生的就是协生的。协生技术也是我们设计生态农业六次产业化专项的一个初衷。在国内的技术力量方面，我们将联合全国 39 所高校的新农村研究院联盟，让大家把好的技术全部贡献出来，进行合作。这些合作使得农业种植方法不仅可操作，而且更加环境友好。在全国许多地区可以由企业牵头建立生态农业六次产业化基地，我们将生物技术和数字技术相结合以推动生态农业六次产业化落地。

（三）生态农业六次产业化基地

我们特别关注中药材六次产业化基地建设，因为中药材对人的生命健康的重要性不言而喻，它更需要进行生态化设计、绿色化转型，更需要数字化赋能。我国道地药材分布在15大道地产区。云南有云药，四川有川药，西藏有藏药，等等。但是，正如食品安全受到土壤环境、水环境影响一样，道地药材的种植也面临同样的挑战。为了实现中医药的现代化，为了守住道地药材的安全底线，我们必须发展中药材六次产业化。那么，道地药材数字化赋能的成本由什么样的价值增值来弥补呢？一个是数字化转型带来的安全质量；另一个是人文创意带来的第五产业价值增值。因此，我们首先探索中药材的六次产业化建设情况，并且鼓励药企、种植基地共同打造中药材六次产业化基地。

碳汇农业六次产业化也非常重要。2021年8月颁布的《"十四五"全国农业绿色发展规划》把"加快建立绿色低碳循环农业产业体系"作为农业领域落实"碳达峰""碳中和"战略的重点。2021年9月颁布的《中共中央 国务院关于完整准确全面贯彻新发展理念做好碳达峰碳中和工作的意见》提出"促进农业固碳增效""提升生态农业碳汇"等要求。

在国家实施"碳达峰""碳中和"战略下，其重要性不用我再强调。关键是碳汇农业六次产业化基地在哪里搞？比如说山东黄河三角洲盐碱地，2021年10月，习近平总书记到黄河三角洲农业高新技术产业示范区考察调研，习近平总书记走进盐碱地现代农业试验示范基地，察看大豆、苜蓿、藜麦、绿肥作物长势，了解盐碱地生态保护和综合利用、耐盐碱植物育种和推广情况。他强调，开展盐碱地综合利用对保障国家粮食安全、端牢中国饭碗具有重要战略意义。[①] 我在科技部工作的时候，当地就培育抗盐碱作物。但是，如果只想做一产，就会亏损，因为成本太高。现在山东省滨州市探索从单一的防风固沙林带、防浪护堤林带朝着带、网、片相结合的防护林体系方向发展，把农田林网、路域林网、水系林网结合在一起，有效降低风速，促进农作物增产10%。其已经对从育种到防风固沙都做了探索，但仍然不能解决成本太高的问题。

2023年5月，山东省首个农业农村领域温室气体自愿减排项目，即农业碳交易试点签约暨启动仪式在滨州举行，此项目在全国也处于领先位置。为什么呢？因为发展碳汇农业的同时可以种植小麦，那么除了可以获得种植小麦的一次收益之外，还可以获得碳交易的二次收益。滨州有大量的盐碱地，如果这样的六次产业化基地能够培育起来，就将对突破

---

① 习近平：《论"三农"工作》，中央文献出版社，2022，第130页。

18 亿亩耕地制约、发展盐碱地生态农业具有重大价值。

此外，在第二章中谈到的酿酒葡萄六次产业化基地也属于生态农业六次产业化基地。这里不再赘述。我们计划先在这个领域推动一些生态农业六次产业化基地建设，探索生态农业六次产业化的落地方案。条件成熟后，可以将其逐步推广到其他领域。

问题 5：生态农业六次产业化专项的新型组织模式

接下来，我讲一讲探索生态农业六次产业化专项时为什么要与中国软科学研究会科技特派员工作委员会共同设计，采用了怎样的操作方式？我们称之为政社产学研融合方式。这个听起来很熟悉，大家听过产学研结合，听过政产学研结合，可能很少听说政社产学研融合。这里说的"政"不代表政府，"政"是贯彻落实党中央、国务院方针政策，全面推进乡村振兴的战略举措。

（一）政社产学研创新推动

《2019 年全球竞争力报告》显示，中国内地的产学研协同创新能力在全球排第 28 位，与美国、日本、德国、荷兰等发达国家的差距巨大，也远不及新加坡和中国香港特别行政区。我国产学研协同创新联盟的平均生命周期约为 3 年，接近一半的产学研合作项目是失败的。政产研合作项目在实际操作中出现的问题更多，其中一个突出问题是在政产研结合的过程中，一开始试点时效果还不错，但当大面积推广时，问题就出现了，最终，项目会变得不可持续。其核心原因是工业化时代重视分工与竞争，在此背景下，产学研怎么结合呢？六次产业理论强调的是生态方的连接和融合，这来源于共识达成和共享机制，要么是区块链技术让合作各方的信息不可更改，要么是社会生态的构建让合作各方认同。社会生态的构建需要有相应的组织行为，因此，生态农业六次产业化的组织行为就是探索利用公民社会化组织进行策划设计。

之所以说"政"不代表政府，是因为合作设计不能把政府当作合作方，而是这个设计要贯彻落实中共中央、国务院关于乡村振兴、数字中国、生态文明建设的大政方针。20世纪50年代，以斯坦福大学为代表的"硅谷模式"是产业界与学术界建立联盟合作伙伴关系。政社产学研融合是一种全新的创新组织模式，我们把"社"纳入进来的主要目的是提高合作网络的稳定性。由"社"牵头设计生态农业六次产业化专项方案，可以营造有利于生态各方达成合作共识的环境，促成合作成果共享，实现合作共赢。多方合作往往会出现背叛风险，造成高额的交易成本，最终使得合作无法持续。对于解决的核心机制，我们在前面已经说过，既要把农民组织起来，又要建立农业物联网，甚至还需以区块链技术支持各环节数据不可更改，形成稳定的信任机制。

在生态农业六次产业化专项初创时期，商业咨询公司无法设计方案，怎么办呢？目前比较可行的方法是让民办非企业单位来做，或者让政府认可的机构来做，比如说中国软科学研究会科技特派员工作委员会。其社会组织的身份决定了自身没有商业利益，不仅可以联合全国 39 所高校的新农村研究院联盟，在六次产业理论指导下提供生态农业六次产业化专项设计方案，还可以统筹协调全国 100 万名农村科技特派员为生态农业六次产业化专项落地提供支持。

（二）六次产业化生态系统的建立

最后我们谈谈，有了中国软科学研究会科技特派员工作委员会这么一个生态农业六次产业化专项的策划机构，有了全国 100 万名农村科技特派员，怎么才能建立生态农业六次产业化基地？我们认为要基于三螺旋创新理论，建立农业的自然生态、商业生态和社会生态，推动生态农业六次产业化基地建设。

首先，寻找农业自然生态技术方。前面我们举过滨州发展碳汇农业的例子，碳汇农业不仅需要低碳农业技术，还需要数字化技术和碳交易技术。根据福建省生态环境厅的信息，长汀楼子坝国有林场竹林经营碳汇项目、武夷山市科技试验林场森林经营碳汇项目、建宁县林业建设投资公司森林经营碳汇项目 3 个林业碳汇项目获得福建省生态环境厅（省碳交办）备案签发，项目总面积为 1.1 万公顷，第一监测期碳汇量为 32.9 万吨。2016 年以来，全省累计成交林业碳汇 283.9 万吨，成交额为 4182.9 万元，成交量和成交额均居全国首位。由此可见，林业碳汇真的能够实现生态价值转换。

再如，福建农林大学的林占熺教授开展的"菌草"技术项目，不仅成为闽宁协作重要的生态农业项目，还被推广到非洲、拉丁美洲等许多发展中国家。

其次，构建农业的商业生态。这里的商业生态是六次产业理论下的商业生态，它需要找到第四产业平台生态方、第五产业创意设计方。第四产业平台生态方，可以从当前的许多平台公司设立的乡村振兴公益基金找到投资，也可以直接寻找这些公司的 ESG 投资和商业投资；对于第五产业创意设计方，我们前面提到的杨凌第六产业创新中心、中国软科学研究会科技特派员工作委员会、全国 39 所高校的新农村研究院联盟等都可以被发展为第五产业的创意设计方，而农村科技特派员可以直接成为推动生态农业六次产业化专项落地的生态方。

再次，构建农业的社会生态。这里我们所说的社会生态，是指在数字文明时代，推动形成满足人们的乡愁、情感、梦想、价值等精神需求的社会建构，或者说形成社会共识。这个共识最为重要之处是让人们以数字化思维引领乡村产业振兴，而不是传统的工业化思维。要让人们认识到元宇宙等虚拟世界与物质世界一样重要，正如"神的公式"一样，要让人们从多个维度认知世界。这样一种社会建构，将引领人类实现联合国可持续发展目标，它不以无节制的物质生活追求来提高人们的幸福感，而是基于科学、人工智能、智慧和创意设计直接提供满足人们情感需求的精神生活服务。把这些精神生活服务与农业、农村、农民连接起来，就会突破城乡二元结构，为乡村振兴找到新的突破口。

最后，这样的自然生态、商业生态和社会生态构建起来的农业是什么农业呢？是未来农业。它迈向与自然和谐共生，是人与人和谐共生的农业。因此我们说这样的农业是健康农业，是未来农业。2023年，腾讯研究院发布了一个我国未来产业指数，它包括信息领域、生态领域、材料领域、制造领域、能源领域和空间领域六个方面，我们认为生物技术、人工智能、先进通信技术等前沿技术的交叉应用将推动未来农业发展。

第四章 科技特派员创新创业

　　科技特派员制度是中国科技人员服务"三农"的重要创新制度，其发展经历了三个重要的时间节点。1999 年，科技特派员制度发端于福建南平，科技部在全国大力推广，取得了显著成效，得到了广泛认可。2016 年，《国务院办公厅关于深入推行科技特派员制度的若干意见》发布，将其上升为国家制度安排。2019 年，中共中央总书记习近平对科技特派员制度推行 20 周年做出重要批示，"要坚持把科技特派员制度作为科技创新人才服务乡村振兴的重要工作进一步抓实抓好"[①]。科技特派员制度能够获得持久的生命力，有赖于适应农业六次产业化的不断迭代和完善。

[①] 本书编写组编《闽山闽水物华新——习近平福建足迹（上）》，人民出版社、福建人民出版社，2022，第 320 页。

问题1：科技特派员制度从南平首创试点到全国推广有怎样的发展历程？

科技特派员制度起源于福建南平。为破解"三农"发展面临的一系列问题，1998年，南平市委、市政府组织3000多名干部下乡驻村调研、问计于民，在此基础上，于1999年推行科技特派员制度。该项制度针对农民群众科技服务缺乏的问题，在保留原单位待遇的前提下，将科技素质较高的干部下派到农业农村生产第一线，开展技术咨询、培训、示范等形式的科技服务工作，并获取相应的报酬。2002年，时任福建省省长的习近平对这项工作进行专题调研后，在《求是》杂志刊文《努力创新农村工作机制——福建省南平市向农村选派干部的调查与思考》，指出这一做法是市场经济条件下创新农村工作机制的有益探索，值得认真总结。

2002年，科技部在总结"南平经验"的基础上，决定在宁夏等西部省区市开展科技特派员试点工作。宁夏结合本地科技工作人员数量不足、质量不高的客观实际，在全区所有市、县（区）全面推行科技特派员创业行动，促进农村产业发展和农民增收，形成了政府推动与市场拉动结合的科技服务机制，培育了以科技创业活动为主要特征的"宁夏模式"。

2003年，浙江省开展科技特派员试点，首批101名科技特派员被派往全省25个欠发达乡镇，实施科技扶贫行动。时任浙江省委书记的习近平对科技特派员试点做出重要批示，指出"科特派制度是一项创新举措，旨在解决农民生产经营中的现实科技难题和培训适用技能，方向正确"①。

2004 年，科技部、人事部联合下发《关于印发〈关于开展科技特派员基层创业行动试点工作的若干意见〉的通知》（国科发政字〔2004〕542 号），在全国范围内开展科技特派员制度试点，围绕队伍建设、服务模式、服务功能、服务载体、管理体制、理论探索等方面开展了各具特色的创新实践。

2006 年、2007 年，科技部联合人事部、农业部，先后在福建省南平市和山东省聊城市召开全国科技特派员"试点工作会议"和"经验交流会"，进一步推进全国科技特派员工作。科技部、商务部与联合国开发计划署还共同启动"中国农村科技扶贫创新和长效机制探索"项目。科技创业创新随之呈现蓬勃发展局面。

2009 年，科技部、人力资源和社会保障部、农业部、教育部、中宣部、国家林业局、共青团中央、中国银监会八个部门成立科技特派员农村科技创业行动协调指导小组，出台《科技部　人力资源和社会保障部　农业部　教育部　中宣部　国家林业局　共青团中央　中国银监会关于印发〈关于深入开展科技特派员农村科技创业行动的意见〉的通知》

---

① 本书编写组编《闽山闽水物华新——习近平福建足迹（上）》，人民出版社、福建人民出版社，2022，第318页。

（国科发农〔2009〕242号），召开全国科技特派员工作会议，并启动科技特派员农村科技创业行动。此后，国家林业局、全国供销合作总社、共青团中央、全国妇联等先后启动本行业和本系统的科技特派员创业专项行动。

2012~2016年，科技特派员工作连续五年被写入"中央一号"文件。2016年5月，国务院办公厅印发《国务院办公厅关于深入推行科技特派员制度的若干意见》（国办发〔2016〕32号）。意见下发后，各地各部门加强组织领导，完善工作机制，搭建服务平台，注重宣传引导，充分调动各方面的积极性，进一步激发广大科技特派员创新创业热情，推动科技特派员工作蓬勃发展。在意见的推动下，全国形成百万科技特派员服务乡村产业发展的新格局。

2019年10月21日，科技特派员制度推行20周年总结会议在北京召开，会上传达了习近平总书记对科技特派员制度推行20周年做出的重要指示。习近平总书记指出，"科技特派员制度推行20年来，坚持人才下沉、科技下乡、服务'三农'，队伍不断壮大，成为党的'三农'政策的宣传队、农业科技的传播者、科技创新创业的领头羊、乡村脱贫致富的带头人，使广大农民有了更多获得感、幸福感"。[①]习近平总书记强调，"创新是乡村全面振兴的重要支撑。要

---

① 本书编写组《闽山闽水物华新——习近平福建足迹（上）》，人民出版社、福建人民出版社，2022，第320页。

坚持把科技特派员制度作为科技创新人才服务乡村振兴的重要工作进一步抓实抓好。广大科技特派员要秉持初心，在科技助力脱贫攻坚和乡村振兴中不断作出新的更大的贡献"[①]。

问题2：科技特派员制度从一个地方的具体实践到上升为国家政策，其持久的生命力源自何处？

从发展过程来看，科技特派员制度并不是指某项具体的、固定的制度安排，而是制度、机制、模式不断演化的农村科技创新创业系统。在这个系统中，理论创新、制度创新、技术创新、产业创新相互作用，螺旋式发展，从而获得了顽强的生命力。

（一）从科技服务到科技创业

南平首次提出科技特派员制度的时候，计划经济体制下建立起来的农技推广体系已经呈现"线断、网破、人散"态势，不能满足"三农"发展对科技服务的强烈需求。同时，农业科技人员主要在大专院校、科研院所、农技推广机构等"体制内"单位工作，与农业农村生产一线脱节。"南平经验"就是通过政府的制度安排，把科技人员从"体制内"释放到"体制外"——市场，为农业农村发展提供科技服务。随着"南平经验"的推广，科技人员与农村企业、合作社、

---

① 本书编写组编《闽山闽水物华新——习近平福建足迹（上）》，人民出版社、福建人民出版社，2022，第320页。

村集体结成"利益共同体"，成为服务乡村产业的重要组成部分。

"宁夏模式"与"南平模式"略有不同，开创了科技特派员创业模式。宁夏当时没有那么多可以服务农村产业发展的"体制内"科技人员，那怎么办呢？其开始探索拓展，只要能够用科技资源带动乡村产业发展的力量都可以成为科技特派员，充分利用"体制外"的创新创业力量服务"三农"。例如，一些涉农企业本身就具有一定技术服务能力，可以引导这些企业与农村共同创新。之后，科技部在全国推广"宁夏模式"，科技特派员创新创业成为《国务院办公厅关于深入推行科技特派员制度的若干意见》的主基调。回过头来看，这是具有里程碑意义的。从科技服务到科技创业，不仅是"摸着石头过河"，还是基于对创新的重新认识。

在传统的产业发展模式下，一项农业技术从科学研究开始到农民使用是个线性过程，要经过漫长的实验室研究、田野试验、小范围试种、宣传推广等多个环节。另外，在这些环节中，部门分割、实施主体不同导致很难实现互动。而在互联网时代、数字经济时代，科学、技术和市场应用同时发生螺旋作用，科学、技术作为生产要素逐步从以外生变量为主转变为以内生变量为主。因而，基于"线性科技创新理论"的科技服务模式，就必然地被基于"三螺旋创新理论"[1]

---

① 三螺旋创新理论详见张来武:《科技创新的宏观管理：从公共管理走向公共治理》,《中国软科学》2012 年第 6 期。

的科技创业模式所扬弃。2002 年是全球互联网泡沫破裂后市场出清之年，而中国却迎来了互联网经济的春天。正是觉察到互联网重塑传统产业的革命性作用，"宁夏模式"一开始就按照"互联网＋"创业模式来设计，科技特派员不仅仅是"体制内"的科技人员，更多的是那些能够把科技、信息、人才、管理、资金等现代生产要素导入农业农村的个人和企业。其从帮助乡村产业发展的外来力量，变成乡村产业的内生动力。据科技部统计，截至 2017 年，全国科技特派员（个人）总数达到 73.9 万人，[①] 服务农民人数约为 6500 万人，极大地提升了中国农业科技化及现代化水平，为科技兴农、科技富农做出了显著贡献。在实施创新驱动发展战略的新阶段，科技创新完成了对科技服务的颠覆。

（二）从要素导入到业态培育

1964 年，美国经济学家西奥多·W. 舒尔茨（Theodore W. Schultz）出版了《改造传统农业》，书中指出改造传统农业的关键是要引进新的农业生产要素，从而提高生产率以使农业成为经济增长的源泉。1979 年，舒尔茨和提出城乡二元结构的刘易斯（Lewis）获得了诺贝尔经济学奖。现在，学术界和政府已经把舒尔茨改造传统农业的观点拓展到改造传统产业，把现代生产要素导入传统产业也已经成为标准的产

---

① 《深入推进大众创业万众创新，全社会创新创业活力进一步激发》，中华人民共和国科学技术部网站，https://www.most.gov.cn/ztzl/qgkjgzhy/2017/2017pd2016/201701/t20170110_130388.html。

业发展策略。科技特派员创业取得成功、不断发展，从自觉的制度设计到事后经验总结，都证明了"现代要素导入"策略的正确性，正如习近平总书记所指出的科技特派员成为"科技创新创业的领头羊"①。

但是，作为政策制定者，我们要问：如何才能把现代要素导入农业农村？这时情况就变得复杂起来。把现代要素导入农业农村，就必须准确把握农村产业发展的规律和趋势。这是因为对于不同的产业形态，要素发挥作用的方式是不同的。例如，在传统的小农户分散经营模式下，科技特派员发挥作用的主要方式就是向农民推广农业新品种、新技术；在农产品加工传统制造业模式下，科技特派员发挥作用的主要方式就变成了企业（专职或兼职）雇员帮助企业开发新技术、新产品；而在互联网平台经济模式下，科技特派员可以成为企业的领导者，通过整合科技、信息、资本、劳动等要素，实现创新发展。

基于对这一问题的理解，我们在推动科技特派员创业时，不仅向农村释放科技人员这一现代要素，还从科技创业、就业角度培育先导性新兴业态。2006年，我作为宁夏回族自治区副主席按照平台经济理念，组织推动实施宁夏农村信息化工作——宁夏信息惠农工程，着力培育农村新兴业

---

① 本书编写组编《闽山闽水物华新——习近平福建足迹（上）》，人民出版社、福建人民出版社，2022，第320页。

态。宁夏农村信息化的发展路径是，由政府建立公益性信息服务平台，带动市场建立商业化信息服务平台，支撑农村信息化综合服务和农村科技创业。2008 年，我到科技部工作，推动科技部联合中组部、工信部于 2010 年启动国家农村信息化示范省建设试点工作[①]，在宁夏农业农村信息化模式基础上，按照六次产业理论进行顶层设计，坚持"平台上移、服务下延、一网打天下"的理念，打造农村新兴业态孵化平台。

（三）从政府推动到双轮驱动

从发展历程来看，科技特派员制度的提出、试点、推广过程都得到了各级政府的大力推动。"南平模式"就是因为"有为政府"的积极推动，才创造了这一制度。特别是《国务院办公厅关于深入推行科技特派员制度的若干意见》出台后，各地方各部门认真贯彻文件精神，加强顶层设计，完善工作机制，坚持以人为本，搭建服务平台，加强宣传引导，充分调动各方面的积极性，进一步激发广大科技特派员的创新创业热情，实现政府与市场、科技特派员与农民、农业产业转型升级与农村社会发展的双赢，推动科技创新和体制机制创新有机结合。

而从科技特派员创业带动乡村产业发展的实际成效来看，其成功的重要原因正是政府在推动中坚持市场导向。坚持市场导向，一方面，是要按照市场规律办事。20 多年来，

---

① 参看张来武等:《第四产业：来自中国农村的探索》，人民出版社，2018。

全国涌现了一批无私奉献的科技特派员，为农民提供免费的技术服务。但同时，更多科技特派员通过创业实现了个人收益与农民收益的增长和产业发展。这就是在科技特派员制度设计中坚持市场导向、激励机制，引导科技特派员走进农业农村的体现。另一方面，坚持市场驱动是要通过搭建平台、营造环境等方式，创造有利于科技特派员创业的市场机会。从国家层面来看，科技特派员创业更多的是通过六次产业理论等的引导、支持地方试点示范、公共平台的搭建、进行经验交流、舆论环境营造等来推动市场化机制创新，从而提升农村产业经济效率。因此，科技特派员制度的成功，可以说是从政府驱动到政府和市场双轮驱动的成功。

随着科技特派员创业从宏观政策方面进入微观实践领域，政府发挥作用的方式需要创新。因此，我在科技部工作时就提出实现科技特派员创业的社会化，依托高等学校新农村发展研究院协同创新战略联盟，发展农业领域的众创空间——"星创天地"，将科技特派员认定制变为注册制，构建科技特派员联盟等社会化组织，实现自我发展。应当说，这些思路和措施仍是今后发展的重要方向。从理论上说，市场主导会出现"市场失灵"问题，这就需要"有为政府"弥补市场失灵；政府主导也会面临"政府失灵"问题，这就需要"有效市场"弥补市场失灵；当市场失灵和政府失灵同时出现时，往往需要社会组织补充服务。因此，科技特派员的持久生命力要由政府、市场和社会多元主体共同守护。

问题3：科技特派员"百花齐放"主要有哪些模式？

（一）南平模式

科技特派员制度首创于南平。2021年3月，习近平总书记到福建考察时，再次充分肯定了南平市科技特派员工作。近年来，在习近平总书记的关切下，南平进一步创新科技特派员工作机制，强化要素保障，搭建培训交流平台，让科技特派员制度焕发出乡村振兴新活力。南平模式经过20多年的实践，在福建省以及全国得到推广，已经形成以下特征。

一是构建完整的科技特派员网络。在市级科技特派员工作领导小组的综合协调下，在县、乡、村三级分别设立科技特派员服务中心、服务站和服务室，形成"主要领导统筹，分管领导主抓"和"部门协同、上下联动"的工作机制。

二是创新科技特派员选派方式。南平市打破专业、身份、地域等边界，从一产向二产、三产延伸，从单一科技服务向综合服务拓展，从节点服务向产业链服务拓展。截至2024年3月，南平市有在岗科技特派员1985人、团队134个、法人7个。[①] 科技特派员大多为科技人员，团队通常由科研机构组团式服务，法人中的一部分是企业法人。

三是为了服务创新创业加强科技金融支持。南平市创

---

① 《把论文写在田野大地上——南平市深入推进科技特派员制度三年工作综述》，《闽北日报》2024年3月24日，第1版。

新推出科技金融产品"科特贷",向科技特派员领办、创办和服务企业发放贷款,并由市财政与省农业融资担保公司共同出资设立资金担保池;与商业银行合作推出"政银担"科特贷金融产品,推动培育利益共同体;对接数字平台建立了"科特卖",通过平台驱动销售农特产品。

(二)浙江模式

2003 年 3 月 27 日,浙江省政府办公厅根据时任省委书记习近平同志的重要批示,印发《浙江省人民政府办公厅关于向欠发达乡镇派遣科技特派员的通知》,启动了科技扶贫工程。浙江模式在创立时以扶贫为目的,在发展的过程中拓展到新农村建设、乡村振兴、生态修复以及工业领域。

首先,浙江模式在创立时就瞄准欠发达乡镇,开展科技扶贫工作。在脱贫攻坚期间,将其进一步拓展为"1+N"科技推进精准帮扶模式。浙江打造包含"1+N"科技服务团、"1+N"推广员包干组、"1+N"乡土专家帮帮团的科技特派员工作体系。浙江不仅在乡村产业帮扶上充分发挥科技特派员的力量,还围绕生态保护、修复,不断完善林业、生态科技服务体系,以科技助力建设森林浙江,打造林业现代化先行省。

其次,浙江模式在健全政府工作机制和市场驱动机制方面做出积极探索。在拓展科技特派员来源方面,形成多主体联动机制,发挥政府、科技特派员和高校院所、各类企业、农村工作队伍整体互动优势,推动入驻乡镇科技服务组织建设。在健全市场机制方面，发挥市场对科技资源的配置作用，加强科技特派员项目建设。通过项目建设，激励科技特派员推广新品种、新技术、新产品，发展有较强拉动作用的产业项目，培育农村产业经济增长点，促进农民增收致富。

总之，浙江把政府推动、市场驱动融为一体，形成了市场引导、科技领跑、政府主导、农民成为主体、风险共担、利益共享的科技特派员工作机制，这是科技特派员制度活力的根本所在。

（三）宁夏模式

宁夏模式的典型特征是科技特派员创新创业。创新创业就需要有法人作为组织载体，因此，宁夏科技特派员中的一半以上是法人科技特派员。宁夏模式以创新创业为基本特征，因此，在乡村振兴阶段，对于科技特派员的生命力，除了政府引导之外，最重要的就是创新创业驱动和数字化转型发展。除了创新创业外，宁夏模式还呈现以下特征。

一是把信息作为新生产要素，提高农业生产效率。在最初的文件中，宁夏就明确提出把"信息"作为新的生产要素，而且按照"平台上移，服务下沉"的模式，进行信息化建设。正是有了农村信息化的基础，宁夏的科技特派员创新创业模式才具有了数字化赋能的新特征。

二是推进科技特派员"组团式"服务，形成科技特派员创新联合体。宁夏聚焦县域特色优势产业发展，组建科技特派员创新联合体，促进科技特派员"组团式"联动服务，助推产业融合发展。

三是传承东西部协作科技特派员精神，借助福建专家横向赋能。鉴于宁夏本土科技特派员资源受限，以林占熺教授为代表的来自"闽宁协作"的科技特派员，创建了中国东西部地区间派遣科技特派员的先例。来自发达地区的专家，带着发达地区的技术、发展经验，助力宁夏实现脱贫攻坚和乡村振兴。这体现了我国的政治制度优势。

以上简单地概括了科技特派员的几种模式，实际上远不止这三种模式，全国各地百花齐放，形成了科技特派员创新创业的新局面。

问题 4：全面推进乡村振兴中科技特派员面临的问题？

目前，科技特派员创新创业遇到一些困难。我觉得可以从外因和内因两个角度展开分析。从外因来看，科技特派员创业的大环境发生了变化。2023 年是疫情后经济恢复发展的一年。中央经济工作会议指出，进一步推动经济回升向好需要克服一些困难和挑战，主要是有效需求不足、部分行业产能过剩、社会预期偏弱、风险隐患仍然较多，国内大循环存在堵点，外部环境的复杂性、严峻性、不确定性上升。在这样一个背景下，科技特派员创业面临困难和挑战是不言而喻的。

但是，我们也不能完全将其归结为外部因素。实际上，2020 年以来，数字经济持续发展，产业数字化、数字产业化都在不断深化。区块链、虚拟现实、人工智能、元宇宙等新兴技术都取得了革命性的突破。科技特派员制度处于平台期，更主要的原因在于内部因素，也就是我们对于农村产业发展趋势的认知、理论创新、发展路径和政策创设等方面没有做到与时俱进。

此外，如果我们按照从事农村科技创业的人员来定义，全国科技特派员应该有百万之众。如何把科技特派员组织起来是一个重要问题。到目前为止，全国层面的科技特派员组织还没有建立起来，也没有相应的数字化服务平台。相反，一些省区市的科技特派员管理平台却十分活跃，如南平市科技特派员云平台，包括信息化管理、人工智能诊断、科技成果可视化展示等多项内容。

总的来讲，目前，科技特派员创业处于平台期，既有不利的因素，也孕育着新的机会。2023年，在浙江推行科技特派员制度20周年之际，习近平总书记给浙江科技特派员代表回信，充分说明中央对科技特派员制度的高度重视。在过往的实践中，科技特派员的互联网销售能力已经得到提升，但是数字化时代的第四产业要求远不止于此。一方面，人工智能、5G、生成式AI、云平台等不断更新，科技特派员如何筛选并利用这些新技术是摆在其面前的新课题；另一方面，消费者不满足于同质化的物质消费，乡村的精神消费逐步成为主力军。在这一趋势下，深入挖掘农业多种功能、乡村多元价值，通过创意设计创造新的消费增长点将成为科技特派员创业的另一引擎。

第五章　农村科技特派员如何打造第四产业？

问题 1：第四产业在中国农村的发展现状？

自 20 世纪 90 年代以来，数据是新科技革命和产业变革的重要力量之一，得益于国家政策的支持，农村信息基础设施建设、农村信息技术创新与应用和以数据为关键生产要素的第四产业在农业、农村经济社会活动中发挥的作用越来越明显。

第一，农村第四产业的实践与探索。党的十八大以来，党和政府积极推动实施网络强国战略、"互联网＋"行动计划等，开启了经济社会全面数字化转型与发展进程。在国家政策支持下，农村第四产业探索实践蓬勃发展、规模日益壮大，成为数字化时代解决"三农"问题的重要推动力量。各地因地制宜，创新第四产业发展实践，探索农村第四产业发展的路径和方法，取得了积极进展与成效。

2006 年，宁夏利用互联网平台思维推进第四产业发展，具体体现为平台上移、服务下沉、"三网"融合、长效运营和创新共赢五点。一是平台上移，进行信息资源的有效利用。从全自治区层面建立农村综合信息服务平台，统一建设涉农信息共享资源库，提高信息资源的使用效率以使信息能够在全自治区层面汇集，形成海量信息服务数据，实现信息资源充分共享。二是服务下沉。依托自治区中心平台，建设互联网电视 IPTV 分平台，向全区 2 万个农村用户提供包括直播电视、时移电视、视频点播等在内的互联网视频服务。将信息服务站作为新农村信息化建设的重点和突破口，以"五个一标准"建设信息服务站：一处固定场所、一套信息设备、一名信息员、一套管理制度、一个长效机制和考核办法。三是"三网"融合，突破网络资源分割体制性障碍。利用现有资源实现电信网、广播电视网和计算机网"三网"有效融合的设想，设计把 IPTV 作为"三网融合"的切入点。四是长效运营，引入信息科技特派员制度。探索政府、农户、社会力量利益兼顾的"公益服务 + 企业运营"建设运行机制，确保在为"三农"提供服务的同时，按照市场机制促进新农村信息化建设良性运作。五是创新共赢，实现信息化的低成本、高效益。

2020 年，科技部联合中组部、工信部、中央网信办启动国家农村信息化示范省建设。山东省坚持"平台上移、服务下延、资源整合、一网打天下"的建设原则和思路，依托省党员远教网络，深入融合农村产业特色，积极探索公益服务和市场运营相结合的"1+N"服务模式，促进信息化与农村产业融合发展。广东省重点推进农村专业信息化服务"政府推动、市场运作"的运行机制建设，推动农村信息化可持续发展。湖南省根据国家农村农业示范省总体部署和要求，按照"一体两翼、三网融合、资源整合、服务下延、产业融合"的思路，探索湖南农村产业融合发展模式。

农村科技特派员充分利用数字平台优势，积极创新"政府＋合作社＋企业＋农户"等运行模式，探索农村第四产业实践。然而，农村科技特派员在充分发挥数字化、平台化赋能农村产业发展的实践过程中，也难免会遇到一系列问题和挑战。例如，战略思维和理念方面的问题、数字技术和数字化营销人才队伍建设不足的问题、产品和服务标准化建设问题等。农村科技特派员如何更好地利用数字技术，发展农村第四产业成为数字化时代的重要课题。数字化思维、个性化与定制化产业和服务、平台化支撑、"互联网＋"产业形态的培育，以及分享、合作与系统经营的思维的培养等都是解决这个课题非常重要的因素。

问题 2：如何培养农村科技特派员的数字化思维方式？

第四产业是以数字技术为驱动力，以平台经济商业模式为载体，以消费者个性化定制化需求为导向，以全供应链数据为核心要素，对三次产业进行深度融合和组织再造的新产业，它是通向"新六产"的阶梯。以"互联网＋"为代表的第四产业与过去的第一、二、三产业都截然不同。第四产业的第一个特征是数据成为新的生产要素。生产要素比如土地，并不是直接的，需要在生产过程中进行处理。同样，数据经过处理才能变成对知识的应用。因此，第四产业就是平台经济条件下，以数据为要素进行信息和知识经营的产业。第四产业的第二个特征是从信息经营到知识经营，不断深化，不仅包含收集信息，还包括对信息的系统应用。从平台、企业到信息知识经营的推进，其间，大数据、云计算、边缘计算乃至人工智能的发展，都是对第四产业的不断深化。利用这些技术，第四产业可以把数据处理成信息，信息具有价值，这就成了第四产业的经营方式。在数字化条件下，直播带货、电商平台、内容电商、小视频玩家等新型业态逐步在农村得到广泛发展。面对这种数字化变革的新趋势，不能"穿新鞋走旧路"，农村科技特派员要树立平台思维、用户体验思维和产业融合思维。

平台思维。平台并不是数字时代特有的"产物"，从古老的集市到现代的商场，都可以被理解为平台。事实上，平台在"互联网+"连接一切的过程中扮演的是"中间人"、"中介"或者"经纪人"的角色，核心功能在于匹配双边市场或多边市场，通过商品、服务或社会货币的交换为所有参与者创造价值①。由于平台供给双方"需求的相互依赖"，平

---

① 〔美〕杰奥夫雷·G.帕克、马歇尔·W.范·埃尔斯泰恩、桑基特·保罗·邱达利：《平台革命：改变世界的商业模式》，志鹏译，机械工业出版社，2017，第43~48页。

台的网络效应就产生了，为平台上的生态方带来更大的产能、更多的消费。数字平台聚资源、促配置、开放共享的特征，有助于将优质科技资源下沉到农村，有助于优化农产品的生产、运输、加工、服务流程，有助于农产品的品种培优、品质提升、品牌打造和标准化生产。例如，电商平台打破了时间、空间限制，全国各地甚至世界各地的平台用户，只需要在电脑或者手机屏幕前点击平台上的不同菜单选项，即可选择平台上任何一种农产品进行交易。"互联网⊕农业"信息服务平台有助于为农业种植、生产、加工、销售等提供动态信息，规避"信息差"造成的风险。农产品电子交易平台为农产品买卖提供网上交易、行情分析等服务，以规避价格波动风险。农产品质量标准平台有助于形成农产品育种研发、生产加工、流通制造全产业链标准体系。

用户体验思维。用户体验思维是指重视用户使用产品或服务的过程、情感和态度，关注人机交互中客户的价值、感知和兴趣，进而给客户带来不同于传统工业流水线制造品的消费体验和感受。从消费者体验的角度来看，"互联网＋"与农业的融合实质上是以消费者为中心、以价值服务为根本的新农业经济形态。随着人们物质文化水平的提升，人们对功能性物质消费品的需求逐渐得到满足，进而出现了对提高生活质量的商品和服务的综合追求。这既包括物质产品和服务，也包括精神产品和服务。人们对农产品的消费已经不仅仅是购买产品和服务本身，在消费过程的体验也成了一种产品和服务。人们的感官体验，有可能从产品和服务订单发出时就开始出现，并一直持续到使用的全过程。用户体验表现在用户对产品和服务的需求更加个性化、定制化、虚拟化、网络化。山东潍坊某食品公司，根据现代人的消费理念，加大无添加有机产品的研发力度，深挖山楂的保健与药用价值，提高原本没有农户愿意种植、采摘的山楂的附加值，打造健康山楂产业园，对外展示传统山楂食品制作工艺，宣传山楂深加工工艺与绿色天然有机健康的食品理念，在发展乡村旅游业的同时，更好地带动山楂行业规范性发展，进而实现产业融合发展。

产业融合思维。产业融合是跨界、跨产业的融合，是科学、技术和制度创新的产物，核心是跨界融合、系统决策、二次经营，最终实现价值增值。在数字化背景下，"互联网＋农业"的关键在于以数字化平台和技术为支撑，把数据作为关键生产要素，延长农业产业链，将农产品生产延伸到流通、销售、信息服务、休闲农业等各个环节，实现农村产业融合发展，并最终实现价值增值。以中药材种植业为例，若是从第一产业的中药材种植发展到第二产业的中药材加工，再向健康产业的药食同源系列产品深加工阶段发展，就将在很大程度上实现产业"接二连三"式的融合；若是在"接二连三"的基础上，通过互联网、电商平台等新技术渗透实现"互联网＋农业"的深度融合，就将带来更大的价值增值。例如，在中药材种植阶段，推行"互联网＋智慧农业"数字化技术，实现水、肥、风、光、温等智能化管理，农户通过手机 App 实现对中药材的智能化种植与调控，从源头上实现中药材的标准化、数字化、品质化；在中药材加工阶段，推行以"二维码追溯"为核心的市场准入和产地准出方式，打造产品品牌；在中药材销售阶段，通过数字化平台，广泛连接健康管理相关机构与消费者，根据用户需求改善中药材产品供给方式，与健康产业、医疗产业高度融合，进一步延长产业链，提升产业融合价值。

问题 3：如何寻找第四产业平台及其服务？

现在农业第四产业平台还没有完全形成，那么我们需要先打造农业第四产业平台吗？还是依托现有的第四产业平台针对农业开展服务？当然没有必要专门先打造平台再应用。科技特派员只要有了数字化思维，就可以学会寻找现有的第四产业平台，为农业创业所用。

首先，构建农业产业数据链。平台上流动的是数据，科技特派员可以利用第四产业平台，逐步构建农业产业数据链。最简单的方法是可以先从平台销售做起，在消费者需求的驱动下，把种植大户、合作社、加工企业、商贸企业等经营主体和研发设计、生产加工、商贸流通等多个环节的丰富的数据资源整合起来。整合后的数据资源可以充分实现市场需求与生产供给的均衡，为合理规划农产品生产、加工、流通、消费提供支持，提升各个环节参与者的经济效益。尤其是数据信息的流动可以将生产供给与消费需求紧密连接起来，消除生产经营和流通消费之间的障碍，进一步提升产品价值。只有将生产、加工和流通等供应链数据与客户端数据及其他利益相关方的数据相连，站在整个产业链、价值链和利益链的角度构建数据链，才能应用大数据技术把市场需求端数据与全产业链各个环节精准匹配，实现网络效应和生产效率的全面提升。因此，科技特派员要有构建农业产业数据链的思维和能力，可以依托现有平台进行这些数据的运营和管理。

其次，推动产业与平台融合。 在第四产业平台的支持下，生产端可以借助数字化、智能化技术，更便捷、低成本地满足客户端的个性化需求，进而实现供应链各个环节深度融合与联动，而非单纯地将第一、二、三产业相加。另外，产业融合数据链的建立为多种资源的接入提供标准化接口，如信贷、保险、客户参与体验等，这有利于共享联盟平台的创建，以更好地发挥数字化平台的规模效应与网络效应。产业融合数据链的建立能够促进信息、资源在第一、二、三产业的自由流动与重组。这意味着产业与平台的融合不仅促进了第一、二、三产业融合发展，还可以在平台上对接保险、信贷、广告、场景等多种资源，从而为农业价值增值提供新的空间。因此，除了产业园区、龙头企业等硬件投资外，农村产业融合发展需要加强数据链、平台化、智能化等软件投资，这种软件投资的核心是能够把产业与平台进行连接和融合。

最后，增强用户的体验价值。用户体验价值是指用户在使用产品或服务的过程中产生的情感和态度，需要给客户带来的体验不同于对传统工业流水线上的产品的消费的感受。平台模式下的生态是一个开放式的生态，这种开放生态既包括用户对产品和服务开发的参与和体验，也包括平台上相关客户信息的共享和意见参与，还包括平台接入主体的开放带来的互联互通，以及上下游企业之间的数据共享等。如海尔作为中国拥有"灯塔工厂"数量最多的企业之一，凭借自主创新的工业互联网平台——卡奥斯（COSMO），成功培育出4座"灯塔工厂"，其成为全球首个引入用户全流程参与体验的工业互联网平台。依托平台用户可以参与海尔生产制造的全部环节，海尔在生产的各个环节实现无缝化、透明化、可视化的用户交互，通过对所有设备进行大数据分析，精准把控用户需要，实现了用户与工厂、用户与网络、用户与全流程的互联。李子柒在短视频平台上播放蒜苗、生姜、大米、豆瓣酱等涉农产品相关内容为何可以如此"火爆"？事实上，更主要的是这些农产品背后的故事打动了人心。这就是内容服务所带来的体验价值。

问题 4：如何通过平台打开数字化销售之门？

吸引第四产业平台下沉为农服务。科技特派员应以联合第四产业平台为重点推进服务下沉。首先，依托数字化平台，实现某一特定区域内生产要素的集聚和优势资源的整合，一边接入政府、科研机构、龙头企业，另一边连接广大农户和消费者。如此，不仅有助于为平台上的各方主体提供数字化、透明化的信息交流、互动媒介，也有助于收集平台上海量的数据信息，利用大数据、算法进行系统分析，把握市场供需信息、行业竞争态势，在此基础上帮助新型经营主体实施精准营销。其次，依托数字技术分析消费者的个性化需求，以需求为导向为新型经营主体制定个性化的营销方案。再次，以平台为支撑，充分发挥平台聚资源、促配置的优势，通过活动展销、商超直销、电商营销、基地订销、旅游促销、宣传推销等线上、线下手段，全方位推进农产品和服务的销售，使得消费端用户既可以通过线上平台实现产品预订、到店自提，还能参加拼团、直播抢购、秒杀等，让人足不出户就能买到健康且高品质的农产品。最后，充分发挥平台网络效应与规模经济优势，通过数字化手段进行产品的传播和推广，在更大空间和更广范围内拓展目标客户群体，扩大品牌效应。

发展新型数字化订单农业。平台作为"中间人"，一边广泛接入产品和服务的需求方、物流运输主体、消费者等，另一边广泛接入农产品提供方，包括农户和合作社、农产品生产加工企业、种植大户、养殖大户等农村新型经营主体，有效匹配供需双方的需求。同时，平台对生产端农产品的质量进行严格"把关"，代表生产端的农户或者新型经营主体与需求端的企业进行对接和谈判，既保障了产品质量，也有效避免了农户规模小、风险高等问题。另外，数字技术和平台助力精准分析、定位市场，实现"按需供产"。数字化、智能化让"按需分配"成为可能。农村科技特派员应以消费者需求为导向，通过第三产业带动第二产业和第一产业朝着品牌化、规模化、标准化、融合化方向发展。在这种情况下，依托新型数字化订单农业，就可以把乡村资源、地域风情和"土特产"打造成真正的产业。这种传统农业的"土特产"本来是"长尾市场"上的产品，很难实现规模效益，但是在平台的支持下，可以低成本、高效率地把供给方和需求方匹配起来，从而形成产业。

依托平台打造特色品牌。农村科技特派员在发展农村产业时应注重精选品种，提升品质，打造特色品牌。特色品牌应注重在优势、产品质量、产品故事等方面做加法，比如，培育农特产品、旅游产品、文化产品等，依托本地资源优势，从特色产业、自然生态资源、历史文化资源和民族特色资源入手，拓展产业链。其中，数字化平台无疑为农产品特色品牌的打造提供了"捷径"。通过"农户＋电商企业＋平台"模式，借助电商企业成熟的市场渠道和运作机制，实现农产品生产者和消费者有效对接，减少中间成本，提高农民的增值收益。通过"农户＋合作社＋电商企业＋产业基地"模式，实现产业的规模化、标准化、品牌化建设，提高农产品质量，拓宽农产品销售渠道，为农村产业发展提供有力支撑。借助互联网电商平台，打造具有农村文化特色或少数民族特色的区域公共品牌，完善农村产业发展体系，进一步加快推进乡村振兴。

条件成熟时打造具有区域特色的第四产业平台。事实上，在平台服务下沉的过程中，科技特派员依靠数字化思维，构建农业数字化产业链，在连接与匹配城市、乡村、政府、企业、农户等多种资源的过程中，会逐步集聚形成具有区域特色、产业特色、文化创意特色等的数据资源，这就具备了打造第四产业平台的生态资源。也就是说，科技特派员首先基于自身在科技和创业方面的激情，依托通用平台进行创新创业。在创新创业的过程中，逐步构建第四产业平台的生态系统，其中，通用平台可能是其生态系统中的一个生态方。当这个生态系统可以低成本、高效率地实现平台资源的聚集与匹配、数据的二次经营甚至多次经营时，就意味着具有区域特色的第四产业平台被打造出来了。科技特派员打造的第四产业平台原则上是连接到通用平台或者"大平台"上的"小平台"。这使得"小平台"与"大平台"融合形成服务"三农"的生态方。

问题 5：如何催生分享、合作与系统性经营？

提升产业融合价值。以平台为支撑，通过数字化手段将农产品的生产、加工和流通等供应链数据与客户端数据及其他利益相关方的数据相连，站在整个产业链、价值链和利益链的角度构建数据链，才能应用大数据技术把市场需求端数据与全产业链各个环节精准匹配，实现网络效应和生产效率的全面提升。以农村医养康养产业为例，依托数字化平台，在聚集农村中医药种植产业、药食同源加工企业的同时，广泛连接医疗、医药、养老等产业，平台在为产业主体的供需匹配提供支撑的同时，还可广泛聚集各参与主体的数据，以数据运营为核心业务催生分享、合作与系统性经营。这需要以数据运营为基础，建立激励、收益回馈和共享使用等机制。此外，还需以问题和需求为出发点。在实践过程中，在可控范围内可以通过先行试点的方式，分级分类地向医疗机构、新药研发公司、金融机构以及科研人员开放健康数据并获取收益。通过对数据的开发和应用，发展新技术、新产品、新服务，建立老年医养康养专业化商城，发展新业态、提供新消费、创造新价值，打造具有黏性的医养康养产业生态系统。

培养数字化复合型人才。随着信息化程度的提高，我们进入大数据时代，农村的"空心化"问题被进一步放大，新型技术人才奇缺，尤其是复合型数字化人才更是短缺，农村数字化思考方式、数字技术落后，运营经验严重不足。应通过新型农业学科建设，进行农业经济专业理论体系改革，加强农业经济专业课程与大数据、信息化的有机融合，以适应社会经济发展需求，培养专业化的复合型人才。应通过多主体、多模式、多渠道加强数字化人才培养，助力农村"互联网＋农业"融合发展；应加强数字化运营能力培训，政府、高校、农村新型经营主体等应展开积极合作，搭建农村数字化人才培养平台，提高农村产业融合人员的数字素养。例如，对于汶川电商学院项目，义乌市商务局、汶川县经济商务和信息化局、义乌工商职业技术学院和阿坝师范学院等多方合力设立电商培训平台。平台通过"讲座＋电商企业游学＋工作室体验＋创业导师结对"的方式开展数字化培育，在电商人才培养方面取得了较好的效果。

建立合作共享的利益机制。目前，农村生产组织模式大多以龙头企业、专业合作社和家庭农场等新型农业经营主体分工协作为前提，以规模经营为依托，以利益联结为纽带，形成一体化农业经营组织联盟。通过产业组织联盟平台，产业联合体在产业链中分工协作，优化利益联结机制，这有助于完善价值链，进而促进产业深度融合发展。需要促进"互联网＋农业"发展，推动发挥农村产业融合的"双边效应"，体现数据要素二次经营的价值创造能力。采用"农户＋电商企业＋平台"模式，借助电商企业成熟的市场渠道和运作机制，实现农村地区农产品生产者和消费者有效对接，减少中间成本，提高农民的增值收益。采用"农户＋合作社＋电商企业＋产业基地"模式，实现产业的规模化、标准化、品牌化建设，提高农产品质量，拓宽农产品销售渠道，为农村产业发展提供有力支撑。借助互联网电商平台，打造具有农村地区文化特色或少数民族特色的产品品牌，完善农村产业发展体系，充分依托电商平台、产业基地等打造农村地方特色品牌，提高农村产业发展质量。

培育系统经营的乡村产业新业态。 乡村产业是开展系统经营的基础。以市场需求为导向，进行产业谋划，积极发展具有资源禀赋优势且市场需求前景广阔的特色产业，加强特色优质农产品供应，满足居民的有效需求。坚持农村产业市场化运作，借助互联网技术和渠道，充分发挥市场对资源配置的决定性作用，加快线上与线下相结合，积极推进农产品消费市场和生产市场的有效对接，进一步拓宽农民就业渠道，提高农民收入水平，缩小城乡差距。积极构建"互联网＋农业"生产体系、产业体系、经营体系，以产业融合为途径，以大数据、云计算、人工智能、区块链等现代信息技术和应用为手段，以电商平台为支撑，推进数字技术与产业深度融合，提高农村产业发展质量。要以产业融合为引领，催生数字农业、电商农业等新产业、新业态，激活农村产业发展动力，加快农村产业数字化转型发展，加快农村生产技术体系变革，进而提升农业全要素生产率，转变农业管理模式，实现智能化管理，提高农村产业发展质量与效益，为农村产业高质量发展提供支持。加快共享农业、订单农业等的发展，加快农业现代化产业体系建设，实现数字经济与农村产业的有机融合，推进农村产业高质量发展。

第六章　第五产业为科技特派员创新创业注入新动能

问题1：什么是第五产业？

第五产业是基于社会新（消费）主流，以科学知识、文化为基本要素，以数据为驱动范式，以创意故事为媒介，经营用户体验价值的创新型产业。第五产业中的两个突出要素引领了一种全新商业模式。（1）数据驱动下的科学智能。不同于传统的科学技术化路线，第五产业实现了在数据驱动下的科学智能化发展。在三螺旋创新模式下，科学知识可以通过数据直接应用到产业中，特别是以生成式人工智能为代表的新科学范式。这一新科学范式，把（技术化的）明知识、（对市场机会的把握的）默知识和（对只有人工智能能解读和运算的）暗知识融合应用，推动科学、人工智能与市场应用的系统性螺旋创新，有效地收集、分析和应用数据，洞察消费者需求。此外，生成式人工智能还能够自我学习、适应并创造出新的知识、产品和服务。（2）文化创意。文化原本是一种无法具体量化的东西，但第五产业创造性地利用文化元素，讲述生动的故事来打动人心，与消费者产生情感上的共鸣，并通过三螺旋创新带来的新商业模式打造和经营用户体验价值。

传统文创产业是指采用工业化的模式，以文化为对象，打造以艺术、音乐、电影、文学作品等为主要表现形式的产业。它通常以艺术家、创作者和文化机构为主体，通过创作和传播文化产品来实现经济效益，如传统手工艺、戏曲表演、美术创作、音乐制作、作品出版、影视制作等。

随着后物质时代的到来，人们将更加注重精神需求和情感满足，追求更高的生活品质。因此，产业价值链的主流设计将发生变化，精神需求将成为引领价值链的重要因素。文化创意是满足人们精神文化需求的关键，也是后物质时代附加值的来源之一。例如，孝心是中国传统文化中的重要组成部分，可以通过创意将孝心文化引入价值链。在数字化时代，对精神文化的经营需要新的思路和新的模式，对于中国这样拥有丰富文化资源的国家而言，探索新时代下人们精神需求所需的新产业的发展规律，具有重要的理论意义和现实意义。

第五产业与传统文创产业的价值创造来源不同。在工业化时代，传统文创产业以"物"为核心，通过把文化要素融入产品和服务提高附加值，这意味着创意必须通过实体产品或者可量化的服务来实现商业价值。例如，一本书、一张音乐 CD、一件工艺品，都是文创产业中典型的产品化形式，它们的价值与商品的物理形态紧密相连。第五产业则以"人"为核心，以经营用户体验价值为商业目的，其不再局限于由物理产品或传统服务提高附加值，还可以通过提供在线平台、虚拟体验、社群互动等非物质化的方式实现，利用科学智能、文化创意来创造个性化的用户体验，满足用户的精神需求。比如，李子柒和董宇辉都将出售的产品与生态自然编织成了具有文化创意的故事而打动人心。因此，这些新型的价值创造方式使得第五产业能够在不断变化的市场环境中灵活应对，同时更有可能触及用户深层次的情感和价值诉求，从而创造更高的附加值。

以"人"为核心的用户体验价值，具有横向和纵向的关联性。许多用户体验价值可以被天然地整合到一起，比如，亲子教育体验可以天然地把教育、休闲旅游、特色工艺等体验融合在一起。在用户体验价值的经营过程中，不同产业之间的界限将被打破。除了横向的关联性外，用户体验价值还具有纵向的关联性。比如，对于医疗健康中的用户，包含健康管理、疾病诊疗以及术后康复管理等一系列不同时间点的体验价值，不同阶段的关联产业需要融合。与单纯以"物"为精神价值载体不同，在以"人"为核心的用户体验价值的经营过程中，用户直接参与生产，消费与生产的边界变得模糊，各种社群网络将被融合到产业中去。为此，具有跨产业的商业生态系统是第五产业经营模式的一个显著特征。

第五产业给传统文创产业带来的一个新要素是"智慧要素"。传统文创产业属于工业化时代下的第三产业，要素仍然是土地、资本、劳动力。第五产业以第四产业的数据要素为基础，以科学智能和文化创意为代表的智慧因子直接进入第五产业经营。消费者为创意埋单，为体验埋单，为家庭快乐埋单，为满足精神需求埋单。因此，第五产业是一个经营精神需求的产业，它不再简单地运作，而要打动人心，使人获得实现梦想的体验。比如，同样是生产玩具，由于泡泡玛特向消费者出售的是惊喜感，因此它的附加值得以提升。我经常举这个例子：你向顾客推销一千元一袋的大米，无论里面装多少斤，他都不会购买，但如果你在推销时把顾客母亲服务好，让她产生了购买意愿，一万元一袋的话，他都可能埋单。因为这个过程满足了顾客的孝心，赋予了这袋大米附加值。

第五产业通过数据驱动新媒体传播的途径，创造出全新的产业形态和商业模式。传统的文化艺术表现形式和传播途径虽然具有一定的历史和文化价值，但已经不能满足现代社会的需求和符合发展趋势。第五产业以数字化、智能化和生态化为基础，强调跨界融合和创新，注重对整个产业链的整合和重塑，比如，数字绘画、数字音乐、数字电影等新型艺术形式，以及基于互联网平台的数字艺术交易平台、在线音乐平台、在线视频平台等新型商业模式。这些新型艺术形式和商业模式不仅具有更高的商业价值，而且具有广泛的受众群体和更广阔的市场前景。第五产业能够打破传统思维模式的限制，具有新的创意，可以借助生成式人工智能，以极低的成本迅速实现目标，从而开拓新的市场和领域。

问题2：乡村振兴为什么需要第五产业？

在工业化时代，乡村的发展往往由农业和传统手工业主导，文化创意的元素相对较少，主要由以下几个因素制约。（1）经济结构的限制。工业经济时代的乡村主要把农业和传统手工业作为经济支柱，这些产业的发展主要注重生产效率提升和规模扩张，而非基于文化创意进行创新和实现个性化。（2）数据要素的缺失。由于缺乏足够的数据支持，乡村地区的文创作品往往难以满足不同受众的需求，无法精确地传递产品或服务的价值和特点。（3）数字化传播渠道受限。乡村地区的信息传播渠道相对有限，主要依赖传统媒体和口碑。这限制了文创作品的覆盖范围和传播效果，使优质的文创作品难以获得广泛的曝光和认可。（4）基础设施和商业生态的不足。一方面，乡村地区缺乏文化交流平台和创意产业园区等重要基础设施，这限制了文化创意产业的培育和发展；另一方面，乡村地区的文创产业投资环境相对薄弱，缺乏足够的人才、资金和技术支持。这些都使乡村文创产业在商业化过程中难以得到充分的发展和壮大。

2018年，中共中央、国务院印发《乡村振兴战略规划

（2018-2022年）》，提出乡村振兴战略的总要求——产业兴旺、生态宜居、乡风文明、治理有效、生活富裕。我国现阶段的主要任务之一是巩固拓展脱贫攻坚成果，实现脱贫攻坚同乡村振兴的有效衔接，加快农业农村现代化建设。乡村振兴与脱贫攻坚，虽说同为"三农"工作，但脱贫攻坚是为了解决温饱问题，而乡村振兴是为了解决富裕问题，包括未来的农业如何高质高效发展，未来的乡村如何实现宜居宜业，未来的农民如何变得富裕。如今，科技的进步和互联网的普及使乡村居民同样渴望拥有高品质的文化生活和多样化的娱乐活动，乡村的精神需求变化与城市并无二致。

作为文明古国，中国的农村拥有丰富的文化资源。文化产业赋能乡村振兴，就要将文化产业中的全行业、各领域纳入全面推进乡村振兴范畴，构建产业、人才、市场和文化资源相融合的发展新格局，制定符合乡村特色的有关发展的政策，积极引导文化机构和文化创作人才深入实践，投身乡村文化建设，展现新时代乡村建设的新面貌。发展文化产业，充分挖掘中国传统文化的精髓，以新兴产业创新模式，推动中国乡村振兴战略深化。

在数字化创新的商业模式下，第五产业方面的创业无疑具有巨大的潜力，它代表新的主流趋势。一方面，信息技术的快速发展和智能化的应用，为乡村实现信息传播、资源共享和产业转型注入无限活力；另一方面，通过构建以文化创意等为核心的商业生态系统，将不同领域的产业有机结合，可以激发乡村经济的多元活力。

我们鼓励科技特派员不断拓宽视野，紧跟时代脉搏。在乡村振兴背景下，科技特派员如果在未来不从事第五产业的创业活动，便会错失第五产业能够带来的丰厚价值。当然，按照传统规律创业也可能获得成功，但无法做到事半功倍，因为其忽略了新主流所创造的增加附加值的机会。

问题3：如何在第五产业中挖掘文创价值？

回答这个问题必须先弄清什么是用户体验价值？用户体验价值是指产品或服务能够满足人们情感、梦想和精神需求，让用户在使用产品或享受服务的过程中具有愉悦、满足和共鸣的感受。首先，通过情感共鸣，用户会对产品产生更加深刻的认同感，增强忠诚度并愿意进行口碑传播。其次，体验价值的形成需要用户的全程参与。用户在产品或服务的各个环节积极参与和互动，从而获得更加丰富和个性化的体验，提升体验价值。例如，LEGO Ideas（乐高创意工坊）是乐高公司推出的一个平台，允许乐高爱好者设计并提交自己的乐高模型创意。其他用户可以对这些创意进行投票，在得到足够的支持后，乐高公司会考虑将其制作成正式的乐高套装。通过这个平台，乐高公司实现了用户全程参与，让用户能够参与到乐高产品的设计和生产。

优秀的文化创意产品不仅存在于现实世界中，在虚拟世界中也可以帮助用户实现梦想，满足用户的精神需求。例如，虚拟现实游戏《模拟人生》允许玩家创造并控制自己的虚拟人物生活，实现在现实中难以实现的梦想。玩家可以建立自己的家庭，选择职业，追求梦想，获得一种独特而具有吸引力的梦想实现体验。

第五产业中的用户体验价值还与社交和互动息息相关。社交平台使用户能够与他人分享感受、交流情感，增强用户的参与感和归属感，如国内的微信、微博、知乎、小红书等，国外的 Instagram、Facebook，用户可以通过在这些平台发布照片和视频与朋友、家人以及其他用户进行互动和交流。社交和互动体验增强了用户的参与感和归属感，让用户感觉能够更进一步融入社交网络。

案例解析：向 Little Miss Matched 学习
如何设计颠覆性创意

Little Miss Matched 是美国一家经营袜子的连锁店，每只袜子都有独特的设计，它把袜子打造成收藏品，激发女孩的爱美天性。先圈群体，再打情结牌；先颠覆，再给惊喜。短短两年间，其就卖出了 60 万只袜子，拥有 600 多家专卖店，资产价值达到 1 亿美元。

Little Miss Matched 的崛起给了传统产业一个很好的启发：有时候，最一成不变的传统行业也许更容易找到创新突破口，也更容易找到商机。它向我们展示了一个完整的颠覆流程。（1）提出颠覆性假设。买袜子时，毫无疑问，我们都希望袜子是成双销售的，而这最自然的规则往往是最容易被忽视的。（2）发现颠覆性商机。将核心目标受众锁定为8~12岁的女孩子，这个岁数的女孩子将自己定位在孩子和成人之间。尽管她们认为自己已经成熟了，却依然喜欢享受快乐，也不在意别人拿她们当孩子看待。（3）形成颠覆性创意。建立自己的品牌，以区别于市场上普通的袜子品牌，以"奇数捆绑"的方式销售。Little Miss Matched 这个品牌名称有三层意思：一是专门研究搭配的女孩子；二是一个看上去并不搭配的小女孩；三是我们每个人时不时会觉得自己有点不搭配的感觉。

如何用商业化的方式经营体验价值？

农产品的文化衍生是近年来常见的一种商业模式，以特色农产品为载体，进行文化包装和延伸，形成独特的农产品文化。例如，宁夏将葡萄文化与乡村旅游相结合，打造葡萄采摘节、葡萄酒文化节等活动，吸引游客体验乡村文化。另一种常见的商业模式是突出地方特色的"文化+旅游"模式，如成都宽窄巷子主打的是老成都原真生活体验，南京夫子庙主打的是体验秦淮风光；人们在西安大唐不夜城看到的是盛唐风华，在杭州湖滨路体验的是"西子景致、千年湖滨"。除此之外，政府和非政府组织（NGO）也努力打造长效的非遗保护传承机制。设立"非物质文化遗产名录",成立非遗传承协会、乡村文化保护组织等民间组织,以推动非遗传承的活态化,将非遗文化融入乡村旅游,打造非遗文化体验项目,如丽江的纳西族传统文化活动、青城山的织锦传承与体验活动等。

与传统模式不同,数字化和商业生态是第五产业中实现体验价值、进行商业化经营的关键所在。数字化不仅提供了技术工具和平台,而且将科学智能、文化创意的智慧性直接代入市场应用中,使体验可以更加个性化,并且能够在更广泛的范围内快速传播和推广。商业生态则提供了一个系统化的商业环境,包括供应链、合作伙伴、共享资源等,使体验价值可以得到持续的支持,价值链得以延伸。

随着数字化技术的普及,体验价值不仅蕴含在线下的各种场景中,在线上也有成熟的商业模式。以抖音为例,抖音作为一个社交媒体平台,成功地将用户体验和商业模式结合起来,为用户提供了丰富多样的内容,满足用户的情感需求,并为广告主和创作者提供了商业机会。这种商业化的体验价值经营模式使得抖音成为一个备受用户喜爱和广告主青睐的社交媒体平台。抖音主打"兴趣电商"生态,通过生动、多元的内容,配合算法推荐技术,让用户在"逛"的同时发现优价好物,激发消费者的兴趣,创造消费动机。对于短视频行业而言,内容生态的繁荣是吸引用户长期留在平台的基石,深挖用户价值是平台企业的重心。

在数字化时代，自媒体的销售方式已然成为农业企业走向市场的新途径。自媒体平台如社交媒体、博客、视频和直播平台，为传统农业企业提供了一个与消费者直接互动和销售产品的平台。宁夏的盐池滩羊，作为中国西北地区的一种传统特色畜牧产品享有盛名，但是传统的销售途径，如批发市场、超市和其他零售渠道往往存在较多中间环节、成本较高且与消费者沟通间隔较远的问题。针对这些问题，盐池县科技特派员强奋林建立电商销售平台，推动滩羊通过供销社品牌和互联网通道向全国销售，探索出一条"养殖 - 加工 - 销售"的一体化道路，引导村民走科技化之路。"直播电商 + 合作社"的新业态、新模式，让农产品有销路，农民有钱赚。

自媒体经营体验价值需要在尊重社会文化的前提下，与用户建立情感共鸣。比如董宇辉，他以独特的浪漫和才华治愈并鼓励了无数网友。他总是用平和的语气，娓娓道来，三言两语便能直击用户心房。董宇辉的独特之处在于他的叙事能力，他能通过故事来传达品牌精神，用情感来充盈价值，唤醒人们内心深处的情感记忆，从而赋予每一件商品弥足珍贵的精神价值。可以说，用户的体验价值与文化是紧密相连的。在第五产业的经营中，一旦经营者或者其代表以居高临下的不恰当的方式互动，就会破坏其价值的底层架构——精神文化支撑，之后，其上层的涉及用户体验的商业价值也就分崩离析。

在商业生态上，大家最耳熟能详的一个案例就是迪士尼。迪士尼拍摄的影视作品的类型繁多，包括各种电影、电视节目和舞台剧等。其产业特点是：全球化与本土化结合，不断创新以顺应时代潮流。迪士尼乐园是基于迪士尼动漫、影片而建成的主题乐园。通过影片带动主题乐园开发，从而拉动园内一系列旅游服务设施经营运转，不断进行业务扩展，是迪士尼乐园的经营思路。除了主题公园外，迪士尼乐园还提供餐饮产品、旅游纪念品，主题度假村住宿以及园内摆渡车等旅游服务，使游客获得完美的旅游体验。

在盈利模式上，迪士尼采用的是"轮次收入"模式：第一轮收入为迪士尼的电影等的票房；第二轮收入来源于已公映的电影和录像带发行所产生的利润；第三轮收入依靠主题公园增添新的电影人物或动画角色吸引游客，而使其乐于为童话般的完美体验付费；第四轮收入来源于特许经营和品牌授权的商品。此外，迪士尼一直在不断收购强势媒体，借助电视媒体的力量扩大迪士尼商品的知名度和影响力，环环紧扣，运作品牌价值链。

案例解析：Zola 的婚庆物品选购

Zola 是美国一家以"婚礼注册"为卖点的在线婚礼礼物选购网站，针对婚礼这一特殊时间，在线上构建一个类似线下的婚礼筹备空间和社区。新人在 Zola 注册后，在网站上可以添加照片，罗列希望收到的婚礼礼物，如厨具、食物、家具等。同时，这个空间将对亲友进行展示，可以发起对婚礼筹备基金的众筹。Zola 以"婚礼注册"为突破口，切入电商的婚庆物品这一垂直领域。同时，其通过引入互联网社交，增加用户的参与感与体验，从而脱离了与传统婚庆市场的竞争，获得了资本市场的青睐。

对目标消费者来说，Zola 最有吸引力的地方在于平台可以帮助他们以一种更有趣的方式讲出一个动人的婚礼故事，然后，他们可以用这个故事去打动那些参加婚宴的宾客。在平台上，用户可以创建个性化的网站，添加照片和文字，或者罗列希望收到的婚礼礼物；受邀宾客可以利用众筹的方式为新人买下这些礼物（甚至可以是一套房子）。Zola 的盈利模式是对在平台上购买的商品收取 40% 的费用，体验类服务的抽成比例则在 20% 左右。当宾客赠予现金时，Zola 将收取 2.7% 的费用。

问题 4：数字化如何赋能乡村文化创意产业？

（一）数字化给乡村文创产业带来了哪些新变化？

数字化技术的蓬勃发展推动乡村文创产业进行巨大的变革。这股数字化潮流，不仅赋予乡村文创产业新的动力，还为乡村振兴带来了前所未有的机遇和无尽的价值。乡村地区的宜居环境和丰富的历史文化造就了形形色色的文化创意。通过数字化手段，传统的乡村民俗、手工艺品、艺术表演等可以得到精确记录和广泛传播。借助虚拟现实和增强现实等数字化技术，人们仿佛置身于乡村风景中，深刻体验乡村独特的文化魅力。这种互动性和沉浸式的体验方式，进一步加强了人们对乡村文化的浓厚兴趣和深切热爱。例如，"数字黔南"项目通过对当地文化遗产的数字化采集和整合，创建了一个包括文化遗产信息、数字图书馆、数字展览馆、数字文化产品等的数字文化遗产保护平台。该项目以数字化形式推广当地文化，提高了当地民俗文化的知名度和影响力，促进当地文化旅游产业发展，为当地经济发展注入新动力。

最为重要的是，数字化的赋能推动了乡村文创产业与其他产业的融合。数字化技术突破了传统行业的界限，促使乡村文创产业与旅游、农业、餐饮等相关行业实现深度合作。例如，通过数字化技术，农产品与文创产品相结合，推出独特的乡村体验活动，吸引更多游客和消费者共同探索乡村魅力。这种跨界合作不仅促进了乡村经济的多元发展，也为乡村的可持续发展开辟了新的道路，带来了新的机遇。

（二）如何利用数字化方式传播乡村的生动故事？

乡村要会利用文化资源讲故事，以数字化为基础，用新媒体的方式去传播。广告是一种语言，随着传播媒介的不断发展，它从依托报纸、电视等单向传递的模式逐渐转变为依托基于互联网和移动互联网的互动交流的社群模式。

李子柒成功塑造了传播中国传统乡土文化与传承题材的领袖形象，她本人凭借曾经的"美食网红第一人"身份成为成都非遗推广大使。李子柒的视频内容主要包括以传统烹饪方法制作美食的过程，或以传统手法制作胭脂、文房四宝与染衣制衣等过程。她的视频有大量展现国内乡村自然风光的镜头，她本人则在视频中穿着汉服，在田野或农屋劳作。《中国新闻周刊》曾评价李子柒是一位现实中的造梦者。在乡野山涧之间，在春风秋凉的轮替之中，她把中国人传统而本真的生活方式呈现出来，让现代都市人找到一种心灵的归属感，也让世界理解了一种生活着的中国文化。她用一餐一饭让四季流转与时节更迭重新具备美学意义，让人看到"劳作"所带来的生机。

短视频平台正不断加大对乡村短视频创作的激励与扶持力度。主流媒体对李子柒等"乡村网红"的关注与报道，也让人们意识到短视频是当下乡村民众进行自主表达、追求社会身份认同、传播乡村文化的有效载体，更直击乡村民众内心潜在的自我表达欲望。短视频成为不擅长文字表达的乡村民众日常生活中不可或缺的娱乐工具和表达方式。与此同时，城市人群通过短视频观摩乡村文化的多维景观，在评论、转发以及与短视频创作者的互动中，表达自身对于乡村文化的看法，也重构对于乡村生活的集体记忆。

除了李子柒这样的头部主播外，国内正有一批科技特派员紧跟数字经济发展的浪潮，利用数字技术和短视频平台，参与农业农村创新创业，推动智慧农业发展。当"歪果仁"遇上中国茶，会发生怎样的化学反应？"歪果仁研究协会"是福建省武夷山市聘请的第一个网信科技特派员团队，这群中外青年混搭的视频制作人员参与了当地机械化采茶、制茶的全过程，并拍摄《不如吃茶去》的主题视频，通过多种手段向全世界传播"武夷山水"品牌。视频播出后迅速走红网络，获得大量粉丝的关注，在网络上刮起了一阵"要到武夷吃茶去"的流量旋风。

（三）在数字化带来短暂的流量之后，各地应该如何经营？

许多网络作品在短时间内吸引了大量的关注，但随着时间的推移，其影响力逐渐减弱，甚至被人们遗忘。如何将短暂的"流量"转化为持续的"留量"？这就需要与第五产业进行深度合作。文化创意以独特的魅力，逐渐成为新的经济增长点。它以创新为动力，以文化为底蕴，通过技术与艺术的结合，打造更具吸引力的内容和品牌形象，为人们带来前所未有的体验。

消费即生活，消费即生产。成都以大熊猫为 IP 的形象延伸，开启了成都元素向成都品牌的升级过程，融合三国、金沙、美食、川剧等特色，形成多元的成都 IP 品牌组合。2023年"十一"假期期间，成都主打城市漫步（City Walk），这一强调随心所欲、慢节奏以及沉浸式体验的新兴概念，与当代消费者强调沉浸、社交、生活美学的新消费理念不谋而合。与此同时，结合"四川游览、成都集散"的旅游枢纽功能，成都将主题游线路规模扩大，打造以夜游锦江、特色巴士为代表的文旅融合项目，不断拓展自身边界。成都的这些做法归结起来，是由传统业态场景向新业态、新场景持续构建迭代，消费场景带来的社交属性、沉浸属性、体验交互属性正在成为人们追求的新主流。

以文化带动流量并逐步转向"留量"的案例还有淄博烧烤。在淄博的宣传文案中，我们经常听到"淄博是工业重镇"和"淄博有悠久的历史文化沉淀"。这些描述无疑凸显了淄博的城市特色和优势。淄博烧烤"病毒般地"在抖音（视频）、微博（文字）等新媒体平台上传播。这些热门视频或热搜的创作者几乎都是消费者，通过他们的叙述，大家感受到了淄博烧烤的美味实惠，以及淄博人民的热情好客。这也验证了体验性是如今传播的一个重要特点，并进一步适应了新媒体的口碑传播和社群传播。同时，这也是一种数字经济时代的运作模式，即通过线上传播引导线下消费。烧烤热潮带来的"流量入口"成为淄博发展的新契机。淄博当地的文旅部门纷纷出战，文旅局长成为"淄博文旅推荐官"，在高铁上宣传淄博，开直播教网友如何品味"淄博烧烤"，更新城市形象，让淄博的热度持续升温。淄博相关部门把烧烤延伸至人才招引等领域，为符合条件的来淄求职、就业的青年提供入住优惠条件和生活补贴。淄博烧烤赢得了消费者的青睐，让无数游客不远千里前来"打卡"，归根结底是由于令人舒心安心的消费环境、舒适的消费体验、暖心的消费服务。始于味道，基于治理，成于口碑。对于淄博而言，"烧烤热"或许有消退的时候，但由此积累起来的治理经验、城市口碑将成为未来建设发展的宝贵财富。

问题 5：生态化如何为乡村文创产业注入新活力？

（一）如何打造乡村文创产业的商业生态模式？

近年来，打造乡村文创产业的商业生态模式成为乡村振兴的热门话题。随着人们对乡村文化的关注度日益提高，商业模式的创新成为推动乡村文创产业蓬勃发展的关键。在这个背景下，一些新颖的商业生态模式应运而生，为乡村文创产业注入了新的活力和商业价值。

贵州省榕江县民间自发组织的足球联赛，原本是村里的体育活动，以草根和乡村为特色。然而，由于其受欢迎程度日益提高，村民们开始将其比肩中超、英超等高级别足球联赛，并将之称作"村超"。一场"村超"的观众人数能够达到 5 万人。作为对比，2023 年中超联赛首轮的八场主场比赛的现场平均观众人数为 2.4 万人。在一个人口仅为 38 万人的县城里，现场观众人数甚至超过了中国顶级职业联赛。在"村超"的舞台上，人们感受到乡村地区所蕴含的激情与活力，同时也再次证明足球作为一项全民运动具有独特的魅力和凝聚力。

榕江"村超"出圈的关键之一是注重数字化营销，善于通过网络平台进行传播。其善于利用短视频等形式向足球界名人如范志毅、韩乔生、黄健翔等发出邀请，并得到了积极的回应。甚至著名的英格兰球星欧文都录制了视频，为"村超"送上祝福。与此同时，榕江开展短视频直播培训，孵化了短视频账号 1.2 万余个和 2200 余个本地网络直播营销团队，庞大的新媒体人才军团、成千上万条视频，成就了社交平台上的现象级传播，为"村超"出圈提供了强大支撑。

"村超"能够吸引观众的另一个关键是利用地方特色经营体验价值。意识到观众来此看球主要追求情绪上的共鸣，榕江县将整个地区的文体活动都融入"村超"赛事中。在比赛开始前，各村代表队身着民族盛装，手提土特产，伴随球员们一同进场，一路上唱歌跳舞。在中场休息时还有各种民族文艺演出，如侗族的大歌、苗族的芦笙舞等。在颁奖环节，单场比赛获胜队伍的奖品是每人两个猪肘子，整个赛季的冠军奖品是一头本地小黄牛，最佳观众将获得一袋本地生产的大米。

此外，为方便更大规模的球迷来现场看球，贵阳在高铁之外，还开通了直达榕江的客运班车，让想要在周末来榕江"过把瘾就走"成为可能。正是因为有了流量共享的发展理念，持续释放的"村超"能量促进了区域内交通、旅游、餐饮等行业的兴旺，让更多地区和百姓从"村超"中受益。

体育产业具有一种辐射带动范围广、产业链条长的特点。一方面，借助赛事形成的人气，立足本土特色文化资源、生态资源、产业资源，着力打造"体育赛事＋乡村旅游＋传统文化＋全民健身"多元融合发展的品牌体育赛事活动，推动体育与农业、商业、文化旅游等产业深度融合。另一方面，吸引有实力的体育产品生产企业、销售商家等落户榕江，推动体育赛事和少数民族特色民俗融合发展，吸引城市文创人才入乡创业，加大"村超"主题文创产品研发力度，形成一条围绕足球的特色产业链。

"村超"的火爆出圈得益于新媒体的助力以及当地政府提供的各项政策保障。然而，"村超"从一场村级比赛演变成联赛的根本原因还是人民群众对足球这项运动的热爱。任何一个地方想要走红、想要出彩，坚持以人民为中心、守正创新，打造一个完整的城市系统是发展之道。"村超"的成功也离不开政府的大力支持。在这里，体育竞赛不再仅仅是商业活动，而是回归到其最纯粹的功能——带来快乐和连接乡土。在这里，全体人民都参与其中，每个人都有成为巨星的可能，每个人都在散发光芒。

（二）打造商业生态过程中有哪些新的合约模式？

股权合约是工业化时代的产物，是为了实现更好的治理，应对企业的所有权与经营权相分离所产生的委托代理问题。股权激励是给予员工股份，股份使激励对象与股东的利益趋于一致。从根本上来看，股权激励本质上以股东为中心，在股权激励下，员工间接实现股东利益。

在数字化时代，链群合约是对激励机制的全新探索。链即生态链。生态链颠覆了传统科层制，实现了组织无边界。群是生态链上的小微群。因为生态没有边界，所以生态链上的所有人都是网络的节点。每个人都是创新的主体，都可以实现自身价值最大化。

链群合约与股权合约的区别在于以下几个方面。（1）链群合约以创造人的价值为核心。链群合约的激励对象是所有人。在开放性生态中，链群主发布引领目标。围绕用户体验，所有人都可以加入链群，人人都可以在链群中进行增值分享。股权合约的激励对象仅限于关键核心人员，对象少、范围小，在物联网中难以真正激发全体员工的积极性。（2）链群合约将激励变成了一种动态形式。在获得股权后，员工会产生消极懈怠情绪，坐享其成。这导致股权激励结果发生偏离。链群合约的对赌目标是明确的，链群也是动态优化的：员工在目标达成后就可以继续跟进，达不成目标就会被踢出链群，被更适合的人代替。因此，动态性的链群合约具有更强的激励作用。股权合约按照股权结构向股东分红，不具备链群合约的动态优化性。（3）链群合约真正将各方联系在一起。链群合约的每一步都需要各小微群拿钱跟投，小微群的收益与风险成正比。这确保了小微群与创单目标完全绑定。在股权合约中，激励对象拿到的股份价格很低，即成本低，风险也低。海尔集团的创新实践展示了链群合约如何在实际操作中提升企业的激励效果和进行价值创造。

海尔集团的财务第四张表

2021年，适逢新一轮战略转型，海尔基于人单合一管理模式，在传统三张财务报表（资产负债率、利润表和现金流量表）的基础上，创新推出财务第四张表，即"共赢增值表"。共赢增值表包含六大项目，即用户、资源方、生态平台价值总量、生态收入、成本和边际收益。其目的是以用户为中心，动态监测、评估和驱动价值创造的整个过程，准确地衡量生态平台的价值增值情况，并展示价值增值如何在用户、链群、资源方和海尔等攸关方所构成的生态平台之间进行分配共享，构建以用户为中心的生态系统。

通过共赢增值表，海尔将表内数据从静态的有形物质资产扩展到无形的用户资源。共赢增值表中含有生态收入，体现了完全以用户为中心、通过用户体验迭代创造出终身用户从而形成一个良性自进化的生态体系。同时，共赢增值表由合作方共创共享，谁创造谁分享，体现的是跨界、跨行业的生态价值。

海尔的数字化转型不断深化，基于区块链技术探索出以"智能合约、技术驱动、全程可视"为主要特征的链群合约应用程序，将原来线下的对赌契约签订、预案落实和预案完成后的增值分享都升级到线上应用程序完成。通过嵌入链群合约，共赢增值表的形成逻辑从企业价值驱动因素方面（用户、资源方）延伸到创值效果方面（生态平台价值总量、生态收入、成本、边际收益）。通过不断和用户交互，其将用户的个性化需求通过链群合约转化成链群及每一个人的目标。

问题6：数字化生态化为何是打造未来产业的必由之路?

未来产业，即生态产业，又称第六产业，主要是指产业的新业态，它不仅从技术前沿的视角出发，如国家在"十四五"规划中提出的，"类脑智能、量子信息、基因技术、未来网络、深海空天开发、氢能与储能等前沿科技"，而且更多的是指产业形态的创新。许多传统产业完全可以利用数字化带来的新科技成为全新的产业。它有别于工业系统，是在数字生态系统中通过新生态模式的创新不断形成的。数据产业是它的基石，新主流带来的具有更高附加值的第五产业是它的价值及利润源泉。因此，未来产业的创新发展需要六次产业化，六次产业化 = 数字化 ⊕ 生态化。

（一）六次产业理论指明了"元宇宙"发展的第五产业模式

元宇宙（Metaverse）一词在扎克伯格宣布将脸书（Facebook）更名为 Meta 后，受到资本市场的追捧。

不可否认的是，在数字化时代，互联网、人工智能、大数据等技术的发展为元宇宙提供了炒作的商机。尽管元宇宙的设想是脱离现实世界，但如果在虚拟世界中一些商业模式充分发展，那么最终它还是要与现实世界关联的，从这个角度思考，元宇宙在未来是必然存在的。

当前对元宇宙概念的解析是有局限性的。在一些元宇宙的炒作内容中，数字虚拟世界好像与现实世界是平行的，它认为工业化时代与数字化时代是两个同时代的、分裂的平行世界。这是由于其分析基础是三次产业理论而非六次产业理论，因此，这个概念没有经济学理论支撑。

六次产业理论认为，未来的发展趋势应该是虚拟世界与现实世界、数字化世界与工业化世界变得越来越融合、越来越紧密，元宇宙是数字化时代发展中形成的人类数字化宇宙。但是六次产业理论还是一个新理论，尚未广为人知。在不了解六次产业理论时，在不影响实业发展，不冲击我国工业化进程的前提下，先将虚拟世界的一些模式做出来，或者实现虚拟经济与实体经济良性互动也很好，但要警惕过度炒作甚至引起金融风险等不良现象。

元宇宙是在现代信息技术的融合架构下，开辟出来的一个虚实共融的经济社会空间形态。其中，人工智能是元宇宙内容生成的基石和创建者；区块链为元宇宙提供可信共识防篡改的机制；云计算为元宇宙应用提供算力支撑；数字孪生为元宇宙用户提供多维沉浸式、高度情境化和交互式数字体验。

元宇宙实现了数字世界与物理世界在经济层面的互通，从而形成了一个高度数字化、智能化的完整闭环经济体系。

其中，数据是元宇宙中最重要的生产要素。在元宇宙中，从数字土地、道具装备到算法模型、数据资源，都可以形成有价值的数字资产，其可以在市场中流转以形成公允价值。数据在元宇宙中上链并实现市场化配置，可以实现价值最大化，从而成为元宇宙中最重要的资产。

元宇宙具有第五产业典型的业态，它涉及由创作者驱动的世界，其重要组成部分是数字内容。用户不再是单纯的数字内容消费者，而是内容的创作者和传播者，从而形成一种基于社群文化的发展模式。第五产业兼具商业和文化双重价值，不仅能刺激元宇宙经济增长，还能带来数字文化大繁荣。此外，元宇宙游戏自带一套经济系统。元宇宙游戏的资产能够通过非同质化通证（NFT）或者数字藏品展示，依托区块链发行的NFT能够作为数字资产的凭证，并能够实现资产价值的衡量和流通。

（二）未来农业创新发展是新时代科技特派员创新创业的主战场

未来农业即生态产业。传统农业进行主要粮食作物的供应，主要满足人的温饱生存需要，在脱农化到工业化阶段，农业发展要解决城乡的二元结构问题。在数字经济时代，未来农业的发展可以充分利用数据这一新的生产要素，农业的第四产业化成为一种新的经营模式。各种各样的平台，如抖音等，极大地改变了农业的经营方式。未来农业远不只追求满足物质需求，在新的生活主流下，人们对农业有更多的精神文化以及用户体验价值追求，比如，健康农业把健康与农业相结合；旅游观光农业把旅游与农业相结合；文化农业把亲子教育与农业相结合；碳汇农业把生态治理与农业相结合；等等。不同的未来农业形态完全突破了原来的产业界限，形成了一种生态化模式。这里的生态不仅包含自然生态，还包括社会生态（如 ESG 理念）、商业生态等。

未来农业必然实施六次产业化。首先，充分利用数据新要素，应用生成式人工智能，生成数据资产，打通农业与其他产业的经营环节；其次，未来农业更需要适应新主流，通过打造涉及虚拟现实、线上线下的、全方位的、动态的用户体验价值网络形成具有更高附加值的融合产业；最后，通过生态化的新模式，如利用区块链，以智能合约打通产业界限，在农业与其他产业合作过程中形成价值的双环账，打造未来农业的商业生态链群。

在脱贫攻坚阶段，科技特派员制度主要解决市场失灵问题，政府通过科技服务下乡，把农业相关技术送到农民手里，推动农村基层创新创业。这一阶段的成效斐然，形成了许多创新创业模式，如南平模式、浙江的"科技扶贫帮扶工程"模式、海南的"信息化推动"模式、江苏的"千村万户帮扶"模式、宁夏的"创业行动"模式等。在乡村振兴的新阶段，科技特派员创新创业有更广阔的天地。我们不仅需要解决市场失灵问题，而且需要解决政府失灵问题，而这需要培育第三方（社会化的）力量。在新阶段，科技特派员在创新创业中，不仅需要掌握农业相关技术，而且需要掌握更全面的新商业模式，其中包括文化创意、数字化方式等。在新阶段，科技特派员创新创业需要拥抱新时代带来的商机，充分利用数字化、智能化、大数据驱动的第四产业，基于科学的创新和基于文化创意而带来更高附加值的第五产业，并通过新的生态模式打造未来农业，从而用六次产业化的更高维度推动新阶段下的三产融合。这是城乡一体化发展、实现乡村振兴的必由之路。

Six-sector Industrialization of Agriculture

TTF's Innovation and Entrepreneurship in the New Era

ZHANG LAIWU

社会科学文献出版社
SOCIAL SCIENCES ACADEMIC PRESS (CHINA)

Preface

Since the publication of my first monograph on the Six-sector
Economy, titled "Six-sector Theory and Innovation-Driven
Development" by the People's Publishing House in 2018, it has
attracted wide attention from various sectors of society. In recent
years, humanity has navigated through some unprecedented
challenges. The tumultuous waves of the COVID-19 pandemic, the
stagnation of globalization amid the China-US rivalry, the advent
of ChatGPT, and the broader implications of generative artificial
intelligence (GAI) collectively signal the onset of the digital
economy era. These developments highlight the need to develop the
Six-sector Theory.

The Six-sector Theory not only guides the evolution of
agriculture but also provides innovative ideas for the digital
economy. Encapsulating the shift from three to six sector
categorizations, this theory presents a new paradigm where the
economy is fueled by digital innovations as well as the cultural
and creative industries. The insights of this theory boil down

to "four new's": a new theoretical framework, new production factors, new mainstream values, and a new paradigm. First, the new theoretical framework emerged in response to the digital economy era which, unlike the industrial economy era, is characterized by rapidinnovations that render fixed production functions obsolete. The traditional linear model of innovation fails to capture the dynamism of this era. Thus, we propose the triple helix model of innovation, which integrates science, technology, and market dynamics within a data-driven paradigm. In this model, computation assumes a pivotal role in deciphering and shaping the patterns of the sixth (i.e., ecological) sector. Second, deviating from the three factors of labor, capital, and land in conventional economic systems, the new factor, i.e. data, is substitutable, shareable, and smart, highlights the digital ecosystem's integrative and collaborative nature. Third, the new mainstream values prioritize the provision of user experience through the cultural and creative industries (the fifth sector). The aim is to satisfy not only material desires, as the products and services of the industrial economy era were intended to do, but also emotional needs. Fourth, the new paradigm is developed by ecological chain groups (consortia) through blockchain and smart contracts. It complements traditional industrial models by focusing on core product and service capabilities to generate a symbiotic dual-loop system. The Six-sector Theory navigates the transition from industrialization to six-sector industrialization, which encapsulated by the equation: Six-sector industrialization = Digitization $\oplus$ Ecosystemization.

Here, the symbol " $\oplus$ " represents a systematic operation.

With the inception and progression of the Six-sector Theory, data-driven industries (the fourth sector) represented by Internet platforms, cultural and creative industries (the fifth sector), and ecological industries (the sixth sector) founded on the principles of integration and sharing have been springing up like mushrooms. However, many pioneers in the sectors were unaware of this theory. Despite their phased success, the absence of theoretical guidance would lead them towards unsustainable practices and eventual failure. The Six-sector Theory sheds light on the rise, setbacks, and fresh starts of figures like Li Ziqi and Dong Yuhui, the differing dynamics between "village super leagues" and the China Super League, the cultural and creative ideas stemming from the online craze for Zibo barbecue, the roller-coaster journey of Ant Group, the achievements of Tencent juxtaposed with its regrettable non-cooperative game with Douyin, and the varied responses to the metaverse economy. A case in point is Haier. Under the leadership of its founder, Mr. Zhang Ruimin, Haier transcended conventional industrial thinking to establish the "RenDanHeYi" ecosystem model which integrates orders with personnel. In other words, Haier stands out for its efforts in both digital and ecological innovation. Equally noteworthy is the story of Micro Connect. Its core product, Daily Revenue Contract (DRC), is the first financing model in China for small and micro enterprises based on revenue-sharing mechanisms. The fate of Micro Connect is closely tied to the logical alignment of Daily Revenue Obligation (DRO) trading

with the digitization and ecosystemization efforts of chain groups. Dozens of conversations with Ms. Deng Xiaoli, Chief Risk Officer, Mr. Zhang Gaobo, CEO of Micro Connect, have reinforced my optimism about the company's prospects, buoyed by its relentless innovation in ecological finance. Both instances highlight the critical significance of advancing, implementing, and comparing notes about the Six-sector Theory. Therefore, we have chosen the format of dialogues on the Six-sector Theory to publish and disseminate this Theory through new media channels. We believe this approach will facilitate the rapid spread of these insights and the advancement of six-sector industrialization.

The Dialogues on the Six-sector Theory is planned as a series that delves into the industrialization (digitization and ecosystemization) of eco-agriculture, future industries, healthcare, and eco-finance, along with the dynamics of data, cultural and creative industries, and the eco-economy. The first volume is dedicated to agriculture. Eco-agriculture sets the stage for stimulating innovation and entrepreneurship among today's technical task force (TTF). The system of TTF aligns with the policy direction of the CPC Central Committee for rural revitalization. Driven by the six-sector industrialization, this system capitalizes on the strategic opportunity presented by urban-rural integration to eradicate a longstanding structural problem in China. The special operation of promoting eco-agriculture through the TTF network is rooted in the development trajectory of the Six-sector Theory, which draws on Japan's practices in its six-sector industrialization of

agriculture and China's TTF system. To sum up, the title, "Six-sector Industrialization of Agriculture: TTF's Innovation and Entrepreneurship in the New Era", not only encapsulates the first volume's focus on eco-agriculture but also signifies a commitment to fostering innovation and entrepreneurship among today's TTF.

The TTF system originated in Nanping, Fujian in 1999 and expanded to include Ningxia in 2001 with the introduction of the Sci-Tech Entrepreneurship Action. Later, the Grassroots Entrepreneurship Action for the Technical Task Force was launched, merging the experience of Nanping and the Ningxia model. After more than 20 years of innovative practices across regions like Zhejiang, Jiangsu, Shandong, Xinjiang, Guangdong, and Hainan, the system now covers over a million experts nationwide. It benefits from the guidance and support of governments at various levels and received official endorsement through a State Council document in 2016.

The innovation and entrepreneurship of the TTF played a significant role in China's poverty alleviation efforts. It has received full affirmation from President Xi Jinping and garnered significant attention from the UN, which has in turn adopted the Chinese approach in global poverty reduction campaigns. As we enter the digital era, the fusion of such innovation and entrepreneurship with rural revitalization necessitates the development of new models, rules, and technologies based on digitization and ecosystemization (six-sector industrialization). This volume aims to champion these innovative endeavors.

This volume comprises six chapters. Chapter I introduces the Six-sector Theory, outlining its key applications and drawing parallels between industrialization and six-sector industrialization. Chapter II discusses this theory's applicability to agriculture and the potential contributions of eco-agriculture to rural revitalization. Chapter III tackles the practical challenges of developing and implementing models to advance eco-agriculture. Chapter IV examines the exemplary models and evolution of the TTF system. Chapter V explores how these experts utilize data and data platforms for innovation and entrepreneurship. Chapter VI delves into the operational logic and real-world examples of the high-value-added fifth sector (centered around user experience) and the sixth sector, providing fresh impetuses and insights for the innovation and entrepreneurship of the TTF.

This volume's content, including questions and answers, was structured based on my overall scheme and years of conference presentations. For certain crucial chapters (sections) and questions, I engaged in in-depth discussions with my writing team. Noteworthy contributions came from professors and postdoctoral researchers at the Institute for Six-sector Economy of Fudan University, along with external experts. Here is an overview of our writing team's collective efforts: Associate Professor Lou Guoqiang organized the manuscript for Chapter I, while Professor Wang Xiaolin arranged Chapters II and III. Chapter IV was initially organized by Yuan Xueguo, Vice Dean of Zhuhai (Hengqin) Food Safety Institute, with significant additions and revisions from Professor Wang Xiaolin

and Junior Associate Researcher Zhang Xiaoying. Researcher Feng Hexia, along with Professor Wang Xiaolin, arranged and revised Chapter V. Chapter VI was a collaboration between Junior Associate Researcher Lang Youze and Associate Professor Lou Guoqiang. Furthermore, we drew insights from postdoctoral researchers Li Xiawei and Li Mingyuan as well as Global Finance journalist Liu Xiaoxia, with the latter assisting in proofreading the entire manuscript. To facilitate international dissemination, this volume was published in both Chinese and English.

We would also like to thank the Six-sector Economy Institute at Northwest A&F University, the Innovation Institute of Yangling Six-sector Economy Research Center, and Zhuhai (Hengqin) Food Safety Institute (Secretariat of the National Food Safety Innovation Program) for initiating the special operation for eco-agriculture. We are particularly grateful to the following experts and professors from these institutes: Zhang Guangqiang, Zhao Minjuan, Qian Yonghua, Wu Zhong, Hu Jinghua, Xia Xianli, Yu Jin, Qian Li, Zhang Qingwu, etc. We sincerely hope that high-caliber teams made up of leading talent in both theoretical and practical innovation of the Six-sector Theory will keep writing new chapters for this narrative.

Contents

Chapter I   Dialogues on the Six-sector Theory

Q1: What is the Six-sector Theory?

As human society progressed from agrarian to industrial stages, economists Irving Fisher from New Zealand and Colin Clark from the UK elucidated the principles governing industrial development. They categorized industries into three sectors: primary (involving natural resource extraction), secondary (encompassing the processing of resources and manufactured goods), and tertiary (covering services and other sectors beyond the realms of the first two sectors).

In 2023, the China Academy of Information and Communications Technology released its Research Report on the Development of China's Digital Economy (2023), which shows that in 2022, China's digital economy expanded to RMB 50.2 trillion, making up 41.5% of its GDP—mirroring the contribution of the secondary sector. This signifies China's transition from an industrial economy to a digital one, accompanied by new mainstream consumption

patterns, new production factors, and new industry models. The transition has also given rise to novel sectors that defy conventional categorizations, notably the fourth (data-driven), fifth (user experience-oriented), and sixth (eco+) sectors. It was in such a context that the Six-sector Theory emerged.

The conventional Three-Sector Theory, set against the backdrop of industrialization, focuses on the division of labor and competition, thereby establishing an industry principle centered around "objects". In contrast, the Six-sector Theory emphasizes integration and sharing, thereby establishing an industry principle centered around "people". Starting from the industrial economics in the digital economy era, the Six-sector Theory moves beyond the linear model of innovation to embrace the triple helix model of innovation.

Q2: What Groundbreaking Insights Does the Six-sector Theory Provide as an Innovative Economic Framework for the Digital Age?

The groundbreaking insights of the Six-sector Theory boil down to "four new's". First, it provides a "new theoretical framework" for the digital economy era. Second, it posits that in the new era, data stands as a "new element" that enables the fourth sector to foster new productive forces and relations. Third, it delves into the human-centric "new mainstream values" as opposed to the conventional object-centric ones. As the Six-sector Theory points out, cultural and creative factors help the fifth sector build its

Six-sector Industrialization of Agriculture: TTF's Innovation and Entrepreneurship in the New Era

commercial value on user experience. Fourth, under the "new paradigm", both established and nascent production factors are converging across various sectors to shape the sixth-sector. Unlike the conventional model of industrial development, which prioritizes equity-based incentives and specialized division of labor, the six-sector champions innovation based on cross-industry integration. Chain groups within business ecosystems leverage smart contracts to facilitate value creation and sharing across industries.

The digital economy is a new economic form that succeeds the agricultural and industrial economy. According to the renowned Moore's Law, computer performance doubles approximately. every 18 months. And the birth of ChatGPT in 2023 revealed the formidable power of AGI. The super-fast innovations that define the digital economy render fixed production functions obsolete and the traditional optimization theory inadequate, thus posing a challenge to the established economic principles. The digital economy has profoundly transformed the landscape of general-purpose technology, precipitating profound changes in economic paradigms. Central to these changes are the significant breakthroughs in innovation models. The well-known linear model of innovation in industrial society, first introduced by Vannevar Bush in 1945, serves as a theoretical framework for understanding the relationship between technology and the economy. It assumes that innovation is a sequential process from basic research through applied research to production and dissemination. However, if innovation were indeed linear, governments could control its process, which often led to

low efficiency. Within the framework of the Six-sector Theory, we have proposed the triple helix model of innovation. This model envisions a symbiotic relationship between science, technology, and market applications. First, science and technology represent two different helices. History informs us that for a long time, science and technology were almost entirely separate. For instance, China's Four Great Inventions arose from practical experience. It was not until the modern era, particularly after the Scientific Revolution, that science and technology began to converge. Their developmental logic differs significantly: while science is propelled by humanity's curiosity about the natural world and results in the constant accumulation of knowledge, technology is geared toward offering solutions to real-world problems. Consequently, the paths to market applications may vary for science and technology. Sometimes, scientific discoveries can directly transition into market applications without requiring technological adaptation. Take blockchain technology for example, the incentive mechanisms of cryptography and game theory are seamlessly integrated into blockchain systems. In the realm of the digital economy, the confluence of science and technology, enriched by contributions from various disciplines, becomes imperative for sophisticated data utilization. This is evident in fields like precision medicine, where the amalgamation of life sciences and advanced information technology (such as AGI) plays a key role. The synergistic interaction among science, technology, and market applications is bringing new industry models into shape.

Data represents a new production factor in the digital economy. The fourth sector is driven by data and operates based on data. Data, as a factor of production, possesses the following basic characteristics. First, it is substitutable. Data can replace conventional production factors such as assets and labor in the supply system. Second, it is intelligent. Data can be integrated into the production process through knowledge systems that leverage the synergies of human insights and artificial intelligence. In the context of the digital economy, knowledge can be categorized into three systems: explicit knowledge (e.g. operating procedures), which is readily understandable and explainable; tacit knowledge (e.g. an entrepreneur's intuitive grasp of market opportunities), which may be comprehended but not easily articulated; and implicit knowledge (e.g. 0-1 codes), which reside in realms beyond human comprehension and explanation, necessitating the intervention of AI and machine interpretation. Implicit knowledge is playing an increasingly important role in the operation of the digital economy. Historical milestones, such as Deepmind's AlphaGo defeating top human Go players and its successor, AlphaZero, surpassing AlphaGo through self-learning algorithms, highlight the growing significance of data. In 2023, ChatGPT, underpinned by big data and AGI, took the world by storm. AI is now breaking into domains that were traditionally perceived as ceilings for machine intelligence, such as mathematical theorem proving. Third, it is shareable. Data-driven industrial models are reshaping production methods and business patterns. By contrast, the lack of data sharing

leads to the creation of information silos, which in turn impedes the potential of data to revolutionize traditional industries. The underlying logic of new industries, such as the platform economy, blockchain, and metaverse, can no longer be explained with the conventional Three-Sector Theory. The platform economy marks a distinct departure from traditional business models based on products and services, as contemporary consumers often access services for free or at subsidized rates. In the capital market of the digital economy era, the valuation of digital enterprises undergoes a significant transformation, veering away from traditional financial metrics and instead of embracing alternative indicators such as the EV/Sales ratio or the Price/Dream ratio. Such a phenomenon challenges the sector categorizations based on the conventional Three-Sector Theory.

The fifth sector, a.k.a. the smart sector, emerged in response to new mainstream consumption trends across society. Danish futurist Rolf Jensen delineates humanity's evolutionary journey across distinct epochs—from the hunter-gatherer and agricultural eras to the industrial and information ages—before entering into a "dream society" where the pursuit of dreams, adventures, spirituality, and emotional fulfillment outweigh material needs in the consumer psyche. Unlike traditional industries that focus on products and services, the fifth sector prioritizes user experience, utilizing digital technologies to blur the line between consumption and production. It empowers individual consumers to participate in designing the production and supply processes based on data. While cultural

and creative industries were present in the industrial society, their digital limitations often led to high costs for personalized design and a tendency toward uniformity, particularly in rural cultural tourism. The metaverse exemplifies the fifth sector by offering personalized experiences within a virtual world. Platforms like WeChat and TikTok have paved the way for community exchanges and individualized expression, respectively, and industries catering to a wide variety of cultural and emotional needs will keep cropping up in the metaverse. The fifth sector's focus on user experience involves the integration of the industry chain and value chain to foster a cross-industry ecosystem.

The sixth sector, built upon knowledge sharing and technological frameworks, is characterized by business ecosystems that prioritize consumer experience and operate across various industries. This sector embodies an eco-economic model, with layers of business networks ranging from the inner ring that profits from the technological capabilities of traditional industries based on the division of labor, to the intermediate ring where cross-industry sub-ecosystems are built upon the experience of specific consumer groups, and finally to the outer ring that features ecosystems or business chain groups brought together by dynamic user engagement and value creation. While partnership-based alliances can be forged in a sixth industry ecosystem, competition may also arise between different ecosystems. A profit-sharing model that rewards contributions is needed to incentivize diverse forms and levels of cooperation within these ecosystems. As traditional, rigid

equity structures often fail to accommodate the fluid nature of cross-industry value distribution, an increasing number of ecosystems are seeking recourse from value creation and sharing mechanisms based on chain groups. For example, the software industry has adopted shared-architecture frameworks like open-source systems.

Based on the above-mentioned "four new's", the Six-sector Theory provides an innovative theoretical framework for the digital economy. This framework can be encapsulated by the equation: Six-sector industrialization = Digitization $\oplus$ Ecosystemization. Here, the symbol " $\oplus$ " signifies more than just a simple combination or layering; it represents a systematic operation based on a variety of tools, such as AGI and blockchain.

Q3: What is the Ecological Economy Model? How Does It Differ from the Industrial Economy Model? What Practical Guidance Does It Offer?

The eco-economic model of the Six-sector Theory encompasses not only natural but also social and commercial ecosystems. An ecological economy is fundamentally different from an industrial economy in three aspects.

First, different sectoral focuses: an industrial economy focuses on products and services. Since the beginning of the Industrial Revolution, industrialization offered goods at lower costs compared to agrarian society (initially textiles), as well as higher-quality goods and services. Put simply, a company's competitive advantage lies in its ability to offer goods either at

Six-sector Industrialization of Agriculture: TTF's Innovation and Entrepreneurship in the New Era

lower costs or of higher quality compared to its competitors. On the other hand, the eco-economic model redirects attention from products and services to user experience. While user experience still relies on tangible products or services, its essence has undergone a profound change. This model encourages enterprises and consortia to understand user needs and deliver products and services that address these needs, rather than focusing on marketing whatever they produce. An ecological economy is built upon the commercial operations of user experience. For example, futurists have mentioned the price disparity between free-range and conventional eggs. Despite marginal nutritional differences, consumers are willing to pay a premium for values such as animal welfare.

Second, different operational models: in an industrial economy, companies stood as the basic operational units, delineating the stakeholder rights and responsibilities through equity arrangements. These equities could be traded on the capital market to enhance efficiency. On the other hand, the operation model of an ecological economy is chain groups. Stakeholders within a chain group collaborate to deliver the optimal user experience through cross-industry partnerships, with rewards distributed in accordance with each participant's level of contribution. Smart contracts, a.k.a. chain group contracts, enable flexible and reasonable allocation of collaborative incremental revenue during dynamic alliance cooperation processes, rather than distribution based on pre-

defined proportions. They also somewhat reduce the negotiation costs often associated with the making of equity arrangements. Under the chain group model, enterprises typically implement a dual-loop accounting system. The inner loop handles conventional financial reporting, focusing on the revenue generated by the original industry through the provision of goods and services. The outer loop tracks profits derived from collaborative efforts within business ecosystems, as facilitated by the chain group contracts.

Third, different supply-demand relationships: in a traditional industrial economy, enterprises produce goods that are distributed to consumers via the market, with consumers and producers acting as two separate groups. Conversely, an ecological economy emphasizes the importance of user involvement to deliver the best possible experience. This is particularly evident in industries like digital healthcare, where relying solely on patient medical records falls short of providing a solid foundation for digital services. Instead, the whole course of medical management and overall health life cycle management requires users (transitioning into patients during illness phases) to proactively share their data. These data, after being aggregated and analyzed, will enable dynamic monitoring of changes in their physical conditions. Intelligent training on a wide range of health data enables accurate prediction of changes in users' health status, leading to a more personalized and precise approach to treatment and ongoing health management

while safeguarding users' privacy. Compared to a traditionally industrial economy, an ecological economy breaks down the traditional barriers between producers and consumers, setting the stage for enhanced user experience.

Since the 18th CPC National Congress, the central government has introduced a series of new strategies focusing on building an ecological economy. These include embracing low-carbon, high-quality development to reconcile economic development with environmental protection, and pursuing "carbon peak and neutrality" to ensure economic sustainability. In pursuit of rural revitalization, the central government has also set forth an array of goals and initiatives aimed at building upon the successes in poverty alleviation to help rural industries prosper. The Six-sector Theory provides fresh perspectives for enacting the central government's new development strategies.

First, the "industrial prosperity" part of the rural revitalization strategy aligns with the Six-sector Theory's integration of primary, secondary, and tertiary sectors. This theory distinguishes itself from conventional industrial economics by championing industrial innovation and upgrading through new concepts and methodologies. The digital age is defined by the data-centric "Internet +" industries, the cultural and creative spheres centered around user experience, and the ecological economy based on cooperation and sharing. As part of the "thriving businesses" initiative, the millions of TTFs can actively contribute to grassroots innovation and entrepreneurship in rural areas.

Second, the vigorous pursuit of an ecological economy, a key element of the Six-sector Theory, aligns with the strategy of low-carbon, high-quality development. This theory posits eco-economic growth on two foundational pillars. The first pillar, data, represents a new production factor that is essential for the fourth sector. The second, eco-social capital, emerges from the cultural and creative outputs of the fifth sector, along with the shared industry model of the sixth sector. Data creates a brilliant new chapter for the innovation era. It also sets the Six-sector Theory apart. In the conventional Three-Sector Theory, ecology was often viewed as a burden of industrialization. Ecology would often be regarded as unable to generate added value and lacks mechanisms for achieving a virtuous development cycle. While in conventional practices, the deterioration of ecological conservation often becomes the cost of industrialization. How can digital transformation redefine ecology as a capital? The key lies in using data to integrate ecological considerations into high-value-added business models. The concept of "eco-social capital" originated from the fifth sector, which operates through two avenues. First, it drives innovation at the scientific forefront, translating cutting-edge discoveries directly into productive forces. Second, it fosters innovation within the cultural and creative spheres, catering to the growing societal emphasis on emotional and spiritual fulfillment, as exemplified by the thriving gaming and film industries. This evolving trend fosters a symbiotic relationship between humanity and nature, offering comfort amid the complexities of modern society. As eco-capital accumulates

through cultural and creative endeavors it also paves the way for fourth and fifth sectors, as well as high-value-added and shared agriculture. With the advancement of eco-agriculture, eco-capital stands poised to garner recognition from both consumers and the capital market.

Q4: What Differentiates the Six-sector Theory from Japan's Six-sector Industrialization?

There are huge differences between the Six-sector Theory and Japan's six-sector industrialization. In the 1990s, Japanese agricultural expert Naraomi Imamura claimed the sixth sector is the sum or product of the primary, secondary, and tertiary sectors ($6=1+2+3=1\times2\times3$), meaning that by extending the industry chain and integrating the three sectors, it is possible to upgrade any sectors and increase their added value. This idea has significantly reshaped Japan's agricultural policies. Based on realistic considerations and Imamura's proposal to extend the agricultural industry chain, Japan introduced the approach of six-sector industrialization in 2008. This approach harnesses Japan's sophisticated agricultural mechanization alongside the formidable organizational and discourse power of the Japan Agricultural Cooperatives, which is able to represent farmers in negotiations with large financial entities. Essentially, Japan's six-sector industrialization signifies a breakthrough in agricultural economics within an industrial context.

The Six-sector Theory also includes the concept of six-sector

industrialization, in the context of the digital economy. Six-sector industrialization = Digitization $\oplus$ Ecosystemization. Here, the symbol " $\oplus$ " signifies more than just a simple combination or layering; it represents a systematic operation. Unlike Japan's six-sector industrialization, we have developed a set of innovative digital economy theories that span the fourth, fifth, and sixth sectors. These theories are not limited to agriculture but encompass health, finance, future science and technology, and emerging industries.

As far as agriculture goes, China's six-sector industrialization is not only inspired by Japan's approach but also deeply rooted in indigenous practices, notably the TTF system. Originating in Nanping, Fujian in 1999, this initiative functioned at first as a government-led service to enhance agricultural technology. It has since evolved into a driver for grassroots innovation and entrepreneurship in rural areas. The system was institutionalized following its proposition over a decade earlier. Currently, China boasts more than a million TTFs, who have harnessed digital technologies, along with cultural and creative outputs, to foster the integration of the primary, secondary, and tertiary sectors within rural economies.

The central government's proposal to build upon the successes of poverty alleviation in pursuit of rural revitalization, along with its push for low-carbon, high-quality development, is setting the stage for the creation of new industrial and business models amid China's agricultural digitalization and ecosystemization. A case in point is

carbon-exchange agriculture, which merges agricultural activities with carbon emission management. Such initiatives are driving forward the exploration into innovative and practical models for eco-agriculture in the new era.

Q5: What are the Typical Applications of the Six-sector Theory?

In the above dialogues, we clarified that the scope of application for the Six-sector Theory extends beyond agriculture. This theory is typically applied in the following four areas.

First, eco-agriculture. Future agriculture is crucial for transforming China's longstanding dual economic structure and helping rural businesses thrive. As mentioned earlier, carbon-exchange agriculture has emerged as an eco-friendly future industry with carbon emissions management, carbon finance, carbon trading, and farming practices rolled into one. Future agriculture is essentially ecological agriculture, by fostering ecosystems through cross-industry collaboration, it aims to deliver the optimal customer experience and thereby elevate the added value of this sector. Health agriculture (health + agriculture) focuses on the development of expansive business ecosystems that integrate biotechnology (BT), IT, health, and farming practices (e.g. traditional Chinese medicine planting), thereby tapping into substantial market opportunities. Cultural and creative agriculture (spiritual and cultural values + distinctive agriculture) facilitates an industrial upgrade. A case in point is the wine industry of Ningxia (Ningxia Hui Autonomous

Region), which now features a grape cultivation base at the Helan Mountains' eastern foothills, and positions itself to compete with world-renowned wine regions such as Bordeaux in France, Tuscany in Italy, and California in the US. To achieve this, Ningxia may integrate cultural and creative factors into its wine industry, including establishing both physical and virtual vineyards to attract tourists and devising commercial plans for wine shopping and other experiences. By doing so, Ningxia will not only advance its wine industry but also generate added value by fostering greater industrial synergies. To sum up, the digitization and ecosystemization of agriculture will provide a new solution to the Three Rural Issues relating to agriculture, rural areas, and farmers.

Second, eco-health. In the new era, accessing affordable medical care has emerged as one of the Top Three challenges facing the Chinese population. In response, the central government has rolled out several healthcare reform measures, like separating medical treatment and medicine, creating a tiered diagnosis system, and launching the "Internet + healthcare" model introduced several years ago, with the aim of building a "Healthy China". Yet hurdles remain. For example, in the "Internet + healthcare" approach, although many hospitals have invested heavily in digitization and information systems their databases are not interconnected. In addition, online medical services are often less efficient than offline diagnosis and treatment, thus placing additional burdens on medical staff. Moreover, these services can only address less

severe medical concerns. As traffic-based medical platforms (e.g. WeDoctor) developed by Internet companies are competing with conventional hospitals for doctors' resources, a synergistic ecosystem is unlikely to take shape. Seeing that the above-mentioned online services and platforms predominantly revolve around treatment, doctors, and medical facilities, we propose a complementary option: research-driven Internet hospitals. These hospitals can address healthcare gaps throughout the life cycle of medical treatment, from routine check-ups to post-operative care. Central to this option is the development of personalized treatment strategies through the gathering of health data at various stages while ensuring user privacy. The overarching goal is to establish an expansive ecosystem encompassing health insurance and focusing on the holistic user /patient experience. Relevant pilot projects are already underway in various places across China.

Third, future industries and science and technology of the six-sector industrialization. With the continuous advancement of digital technologies, big data, cloud computing, blockchain, and AGI have emerged in recent years, alongside new industry forms like the metaverse. These innovations stem from the expansion of the digital economy, and their economic implications need to be examined through the lens of innovation economics. Digital tools and industries are predominantly data-driven. Some, like the metaverse, build their business models upon user experience. The development of these tools and industries would be impossible without a cross-

industry ecosystem.

Take blockchain for example. Blockchain is more than just a technology or a collection of technologies; it is the cornerstone of business ecosystems. The fact that Bitcoin was born before blockchain indicates that a blockchain business and technology ecosystem should be built upon existing application scenarios. The sixth sector is the key arena for blockchain's growth. Blockchain thrives on fitting application scenarios that unlock its potential benefits. Absent these scenarios, it becomes a cost-burdened, intricate technology with no real-world utility. The sixth sector, a.k.a. the shared sector, features a system of interconnected industrial segments, which is similar to blockchain's structure. Blockchain intertwines science, technology, and application scenarios into helices. It needs an arena to harness its core technologies such as smart contracts, asymmetric encryption, and consensus mechanisms. Blockchain's attributes of tamper-resistance and decentralization address trust concerns and facilitate partnerships within the sixth sector. Technically speaking, blockchain offers a sophisticated operational framework to tackle the challenge of sharing. Guided by the Six-sector Theory, blockchain can identify and leverage fitting application scenarios. Additionally, blockchain fosters an ecosystem of cultural and creative sharing.

The much-hyped metaverse posits the coexistence of the virtual and physical worlds, implying that the industrial and digital ages are unfolding concurrently. This idea is anchored in the Three-

Sector Theory. In contrast, the Six-sector Theory argues against dividing the world into two parallel realms. Instead, it envisions a future where the virtual and physical worlds, i.e. the digital and industrial sectors, are increasingly interconnected. The metaverse is a digitized universe emerging from the development of the digital age. The metaverse industry needs to explore commercial possibilities that enhance user experience, thereby developing business ecosystems to foster business and industrial innovation based on digitization and ecosystemization.

Fourth, eco-finance. Eco-finance utilizes blockchain and smart contracts to forge an ecological model for finance. Traditional finance relies on equity arrangements, wherein an entity's future cash flows are forecast using financial statements. Such forecasts in turn provide the basis for valuation and transactional decision-making. In contrast, the eco-finance model supports businesses that exhibit commercial viability yet lack the financing tools needed for expansion. It helps these businesses build ecosystems and create value together, and share their rewards through smart contracts. A typical example of eco-finance in its early stages is Micro Connect. This startup focuses on investing in small and micro businesses. Instead of creating equity or debt relationships, it embraces collaborative entrepreneurship and post-expansion profit-sharing facilitated by smart contracts. This strategy has yielded notable success, with over 10000 stores now covered by Micro Connect's smart contract framework. Additionally, Micro Connect's listing on the Macao Financial Assets Exchange signals its securitization

and debut in the primary capital market. Micro Connect's practice has set a precedent for eco-finance. However, the market viability warrants ongoing assessment.

Chapter II   Six-sector Industrialization of Agriculture

Q1: What are the Main Challenges Facing the Agricultural Modernization and Rural Revitalization of China?

President Xi Jinping noted that future endeavors in "San Nong" (agriculture, rural areas, and farmers) should prioritize the holistic advancement of rural revitalization. The overarching aim is to achieve agricultural modernization by 2035 and establish China as an agricultural powerhouse by the mid-21st century.[1] We share the commitment of developed countries to ensuring food security, increasing farmers' incomes, narrowing the urban-rural gap, and realizing sustainable agricultural and rural development. However, the national circumstances of China set it apart from the developed world. The challenges we encounter in modernizing agriculture and rejuvenating rural areas are distinctive. Addressing these challenges

---

[1]   习近平:《加快建设农业强国　推进农业农村现代化》,《求是》2023 年第 6 期。

entails not the direct emulation of foreign models but the implementation of strategies tailored to China's realities.

First, the agricultural modernization of China is defined by the prevalence of smallholder family farming. This approach is rooted in the demographic challenge posed by a vast population with scarce arable land. According to the third agricultural census, over 98% of agricultural operators are smallholder families, each managing an average of 7.8 mu (approx. 0.52 hectare). These small farms represent 70% of China's total cultivated area[①], presenting a sharp contrast to the ranching business in the US. For China, the key tasks include enhancing the incomes of small-scale farmers, safeguarding national food security, and narrowing the urban-rural divide, all under the constraints of limited agricultural resources. Central to the strategy for agricultural modernization is the commitment to keeping "Chinese people's rice bowls firmly in their own hands".

Second, China follows a green path to agricultural modernization. Facing the dual pressures of a large population and scarce land resources, China has traditionally leaned on chemical aids such as fertilizers, pesticides, and preservatives to boost agricultural output. This approach, however, has precipitated adverse effects, including soil degradation, contamination, and food safety crises, notably the 2008 "Tainted Milk" scandal which spurred a global hunt for safer infant formula by Chinese consumers. The

---

① 《第三次全国农业普查主要数据公报（第一号）》, https://www.gov.cn/xinwen/2017-12/14/content_5246817.htm。

Six-sector Industrialization of Agriculture: TTF's Innovation and Entrepreneurship in the New Era

lesson is clear: no compromise is too small in the realm of food safety. In fact, the repercussions of this approach extend beyond soil degradation to water and air pollution, diminished biodiversity, and a rise in natural disasters due to climate change, all underscoring the need for sustainable development. It is evident that the old path is untenable. Instead, we need to reduce chemical use in farming and safeguard natural ecosystems. The challenge lies in how to catalyze the green transformation of China's agricultural sector with advanced technology. We aim to achieve agricultural modernization in the pursuit of carbon peak and neutrality. In contrast, when the US, the EU, and Japan initiated agricultural modernization, these goals were not yet established.

Third, China strives to balance urban and rural development while progressing towards agricultural modernization. The quest for common prosperity in China is hindered by three main disparities: regional differences, the urban-rural divide, and inequalities among various social groups. The disparity between modern cities and underdeveloped rural areas is particularly stark in China, compared to that of developed nations. It has created a stable yet daunting dual structure, one that persists despite decades of attempts to bridge it. Although China's urbanization rate approaches 65%, the remaining 35% of the population residing in rural areas represents a considerable demographic, especially in a country with a population of 1.4 billion. Since the inception of the reform and opening-up, the nation has been committed to poverty alleviation, rural

revitalization, and the reduction of the urban-rural divide. The industrialization and urbanization processes have facilitated a transition of labor from agricultural to non-agricultural sectors, accompanied by the migration of farmers to cities, thereby fostering opportunities for agricultural modernization and rural revitalization. These obstacles are particularly pronounced in the underdeveloped western regions, where the aforementioned disparities often converge. Compounded by an aging population and the reliance on rural areas for both employment and elder care, the revitalization of rural communities remains a pressing concern.

Fourth, China's agricultural modernization unfolds in the era of digital civilization. As we have discussed, agricultural modernization in developed economies like the US, the EU, and Japan was accompanied by industrialization and urbanization. Contrarily, China's journey towards agricultural modernization coincides with the global transition into the digital civilization era. This new era allows us and data platforms, among other assets within the digital economy, to transform, consolidate, and modernize agriculture. In other words, the absence of agricultural conditions akin to those in the US or the EU does not equate to a lack of alternatives; instead, the digital economy unveils a fresh avenue for agricultural modernization in China. The essence of eco-agriculture lies in utilizing data as a new factor to foster new paradigms for the fourth, fifth, and sixth sectors, and align with the new mainstream values centered around personal well-

being and emotional fulfillment. Consequently, capitalizing on the technologies birthed by digital civilization to pave novel pathways for the integrated development of rural areas and the symbiosis of urban and rural industries represents both a challenge and an opportunity for us.

Q2: What is the Six-sector Industrialization of Agriculture?

Let's first discuss the concepts of natural ecosystem, business ecosystem, and social ecosystem, before exploring the six-sector industrialization of agriculture and the necessity of eco-agriculture for China.

(I) Natural Ecosystem, Business Ecosystem, and Social Ecosystem

The digitally empowered agricultural modernization has fostered growth within natural, business, and social ecosystems.

First, honor the principles governing natural ecosystems while promoting the comprehensive green transformation of rural industries. Natural ecosystems consist of living organisms and non-living elements that interact within the environment, functioning as an organic whole through a series of physical, chemical, and biological processes. Each component of a natural ecosystem is directly or indirectly connected, rather than operating in isolation. While industrial innovations have been introduced into natural ecosystems to boost agricultural productivity, excessive manipulation could lead to various challenges, such as heightened concerns regarding food safety and the spread of food-borne illnesses.

As the Report to the 20th CPC National Congress pointed out, "Respecting, adapting to, and protecting nature is essential for building China into a modern socialist country in all respects". Adhering to the belief that lucid waters and lush mountains are invaluable assets, China should incorporate the vision of harmonious coexistence between humanity and nature into its plan for the rejuvenation of rural industries. Guided by the principle of green development and the "dual carbon" goals, China must direct its agricultural modernization efforts towards the green transformation of rural industries. This transformation necessitates robust measures for safeguarding agricultural resources and rural environments. Specifically, China should strive to address salinization, soil erosion, and heavy metal contamination of arable land, and adopt water-saving irrigation technologies to curtail resource depletion. Additionally, it should safeguard and revitalize natural ecosystems to preserve biodiversity within agricultural settings. A third approach is to establish a low-carbon rural industrial system, develop mechanisms for realizing the value of eco-friendly products, and strengthen the environmental compensation rules. Most importantly, the green transformation of rural industries should be bolstered by digitization. Accessible, accurate, and affordable data underpins the realization of ecological value and lays the foundation for carbon accounting and trading.

Sony Computer Science Laboratories (Sony CSL) has developed an agricultural technology to address environmental concerns, food

hygiene, poverty, and other societal issues. Known as "Symbiotic Agriculture", this technology replaces monoculture with dense intercropping. It eliminates the need for tilling, fertilization, and pesticide application, and relies instead on the interactions among a variety of plants and between crops and the environment to foster a naturally ordered ecosystem. Symbiotic Agriculture significantly contributes to the fulfillment of sustainable development goals by tackling global issues such as environmental degradation, substandard food, and poverty. Sony China has partnered with local companies to deploy this technology in Wuxi, Huizhou, Suzhou, and other places. As a pioneering effort in biodiversity conservation, Symbiotic Agriculture explores viable methods for fostering harmonious coexistence between humans and nature while maintaining ecological balance. While Symbiotic Agriculture may not definitively assert itself as the future of farming, it presents a compelling alternative to agricultural industrialization.

Second, adapt to the digital economy's development patterns and foster business ecosystems for rural revitalization. In the era of industrialization, agriculture, characterized by low added value and intensive labor requirements, was positioned at the upper stream of the industrial chain. Agricultural industrialization adhered to the principles of division of labor and market competition. According to the Core-Periphery Theory of Development Economics, cities thrived at the cost of agriculture and rural areas. The digital economy offers an opportunity to dismantle this "dual

structure" by fostering business ecosystems for rural industries. These ecosystems focus not on agricultural products but on "lifetime user experience". Central to the digital economy is the concept of user value, which is amplified by platforms through the creation of "digital profiles" that aim to enhance user experience and stickiness. While adhering to the traditional model of division of labor and market competition, the digital economy era also advocates for cooperation and integration. This is evident in the transition from "supplier contracts" between upper- and lower-stream entities along the agricultural supply chains to "ecosystem contracts" or "chain group contracts", which are founded on the principles of cooperation and integration rather than division of labor and market competition. Partners within ecosystems and chain groups are committed to jointly creating lifetime value for users and sharing the new value added. Therefore, to rejuvenate rural industries, it is imperative to view farmers and new agricultural operators as partners and work with them to develop business ecosystems that distribute the additional benefits of modernization.

The development of Ningxia Yanchi Tan-Sheep Industry Group is a typical case of refining a business ecosystem through brand building. The company meticulously monitors the high-end market, capitalizing on significant international and domestic conferences to broaden its reach with the help of business and government partners. It encourages enterprises along the industry chain to develop new products by "providing rewards instead of subsidies" and participate in agri-product trade fairs, with the aim of enhancing

independent marketing efforts and exploring new markets. Riding the momentum of major conferences and exhibitions, including the G20 Summit, BRICS Summit, SCO Summit, and Davos Forum in Dalian, the company organized branding events for "Yanchi Tan Sheep" in large- and medium-sized cities such as Hangzhou, Shenzhen, Shanghai, and Beijing. These events featured executives from leading catering companies, upscale hotels, malls, and trading and logistics organizations. Through sustained efforts in branding, Yanchi Tan-Sheep Industry Group has elevated its regional brand value to over RMB 7 billion, earning widespread acclaim across society and elevating the entire industry to new heights. This underscores the vital impact of creative brand design on eco-agriculture.

Third, expand the application of digital technologies to build social ecosystems for agricultural modernization. With the development of digital technologies such as augmented reality and virtual reality, cyberspace is redefining social ecosystems. "AI digital humans" have carved out a new niche as live-streaming products. Social networks, shopping platforms, virtual communities and scenarios, and the forthcoming metaverse have brought profound changes to the physical rural spaces. Representing a fusion of the physical and digital worlds, rural areas are set to become a key backdrop for future living. Rural social ecosystems encompass more than the relationship between humans and nature; they provide expansive opportunities for progress in education, healthcare, eldercare, biodiversity

conservation, food security, and efforts to mitigate climate change. Their evolution is steered by both the progress in digital technologies and the direction of public policies. Although the social ecosystems for agricultural modernization are still in their early stages, they hold the potential to profoundly impact rural areas. To drive national development through agriculture and realize the common prosperity of farmers and rural areas, China needs to proactively foster social ecosystems for agricultural modernization.

(II) Six-sector Industrialization of Agriculture

The six-sector industrialization of agriculture signifies the development of future agriculture or health agriculture. It focuses on delivering eco-friendly products and services to bolster human health. The purposes of health agriculture range from offering healthy and nutritious food to promoting the planet's well-being and the sustainable development of humanity. These purposes are intrinsically tied to the natural, business, and social ecosystems that we have mentioned before. The core focus of the six-sector industrialization is on eco-agriculture, meaning that China's agricultural modernization should follow ecological principles and embrace a green pathway. Furthermore, China's agricultural modernization should explore new avenues within the digital economy's business and social ecosystems. The building of these ecosystems, along with the pursuit of green development, are key to increasing farmers' incomes.

As climate change looms large, humanity is facing severe

sustainability challenges, particularly in the realm of agriculture. On September 22, 2020, President Xi Jinping solemnly announced to the world at the general debate of the 75th session of the UN General Assembly that "China will scale up its Intended Nationally Determined Contributions by adopting more vigorous policies and measures, and aims to have CO_2 emissions peak before 2030 and achieve carbon neutrality before 2060". The commitment to achieving the "dual carbon" goals necessitates the in-depth implementation of the eco-civilization concept and the pursuit of green development. Under the guiding framework of building eco-civilization, China prioritizes the integrated development of agriculture-related industries. As organic agriculture, modern food processing bases, agricultural parks, eco-farms, and rural cultural tourism are thriving across the country, the agricultural production and distribution processes are improving by the day, bringing into shape a preliminary industry chain where the primary, secondary, and tertiary sectors converge.

From the perspective of health agriculture, it is also essential to properly manage the human relationships with society and nature. Human health is not just about physical and mental well-being; it also involves the functionality of society and the balance between humans and nature. In today's digital economy, marked by rapid advancements in robotics and AI, much physical and some intellectual labor is being automated. ChatGPT is a prime example of this trend. This shift calls for a reevaluation of the human-society dynamics. Farmers are facing comparable challenges,

which prompts the agricultural sector to reconsider the relationship between humans and nature. One possible cause of the COVID-19 pandemic is the disruptions in the human-nature nexus. Moreover, the rising global temperature is causing more frequent extreme weather events, which not only concern scientists but also directly affect the survival of every individual.

The six-sector industrialization involves adhering to the natural laws of agriculture and employing technologies and theories for the digital economy to create business ecosystems that focus on lifetime user experience, and on such basis gradually foster social ecosystems that bridge the gap between urban and rural communities. Modern agriculture needs to fully unleash the advantages of the data-driven fourth sector to merge primary, secondary, and tertiary sectors in rural areas and create new industry models. It should also combine cultural, creative, and intelligent elements to design rural and urban-rural industries, thereby exploring the fifth sector. China's future agriculture ought to be developed through the fusion of the primary, secondary, tertiary, fourth, and fifth sectors. This forms the basic conceptual framework of eco-agriculture.

(III) The Logic of Eco-agriculture

I would like to briefly explain the logic of eco-agriculture from four aspects. Subsequently, a chapter will be dedicated to the specialized operations concerned, with the goal of offering both theoretical insights and practical advice for the six-sector industrialization of agriculture.

First, eco-agriculture refers to agricultural modernization in the era of digital civilization. In contrast, an industrial civilization was characterized by a distinct division of labor, market competition, and a focus on products. Back then, agriculture was at the top of the industry chain, supplying raw materials to the food, chemical, and textile industries. Consequently, farmers received the lowest share of benefits along the entire chain. Against this backdrop, Japan embarked on integrating industry and services into rural areas, aiming to boost rural productivity and combat rural decline. When it comes to the six-sector industrialization, San Nong is regarded as a partner of business ecosystems that focus on lifetime user experience. Partners are expected to mingle and share —mingling into an ecosystem and sharing its values. From an economic standpoint, this signifies a departure from the industrial age. The introduction of the tractor in 1900 marked the onset of the first agricultural revolution, which significantly enhanced agricultural productivity and brought substantial benefits to countries like the US, the UK, and France. The second agricultural revolution was driven by advancements in fertilizers, pesticides, and preservation methods, particularly the incorporation of modern biotechnology into farming practices. Now, as we enter the digital civilization era, agriculture stands on the cusp of a third revolution.

Second, eco-agriculture is oriented towards lifetime user experience. Lifetime user experience epitomizes a people-centric development strategy. Agriculture extends beyond offering a singular

product experience; it intertwines with cultural tourism and recreation, providing opportunities for natural and rural sightseeing. Furthermore, it serves as a platform for civilizational education and promotion. The specific experience that agriculture delivers should be systematically designed in line with customer needs. With constant experience come constant transactions and constant benefits for farmers. Li Ziqi's live-streamed content embodies a new and meticulously industry-university-research rooted in rural living. At the heart of this content offering lies the perception of the intrinsic value of user experience. Li Ziqi's culinary videos showcase the natural ecosystems, the growth, collection, and processing of farm produce, and rural cooking techniques inspired by Sichuan cuisine. These videos offer city dwellers a bridge to nature and rural society, evoking a nostalgic longing. They stand as prime examples of how creative endeavors can drive rural rejuvenation through eco-agriculture.

Third, eco-agriculture relies on ecological contracts. Unlike procurement contracts between upper- and lower-stream entities within an industrial economy, which reduce transaction costs by specifying standardized product information such as the subject matter and quality requirements, ecological contracts are premised on long-term benefits driven by user experience. The key lies in forming symbiotic ecosystems, symbiotic organizational models, and symbiotic behavioral patterns. These "three symbiotic's" are crucial for an eco-agricultural system. The halting of Li Ziqi's programming since July 2021 resulted from a breach in ecological

contracts or, to be precise, a breakdown in the mutually supporting environment and organizational framework. Ecological contracts introduce a novel business paradigm in the digital era, necessitating specialized training and a systematic approach to forge the "three symbiotic's" and ensure the sustainability of business ecosystems. The essence of ecological contract design lies in identifying eco-partners, thereby avoiding the need to build everything anew.

Fourth, eco-agriculture runs through industrial organizations under the chain group model. As mentioned above, symbiotic organizations are also known as "industrial chain groups". An industrial economy focused on products and services and operated through equity structures. During the industrial economy era, numerous entrepreneurs adopted a winner-takes-all mentality in pursuit of dominant market positions, relegating minority shareholders to peripheral roles within their companies' equity structures. This concentration of power frequently resulted in a monopoly. In contrast, an ecological economy shifts its focus away from equity structures towards chain group structures. A chain group structure refers to a networked organizational model that prioritizes lifetime user experience. In this model, anyone who contributes value to users is recognized as eco-partners. The relationships with eco-partners are managed through digital chain groups, facilitated by specific contracts or consortia. This approach is feasible in the context of blockchain and third-generation Internet(web3.0), which offer higher efficiency and security for

executing chain group contracts than equity structures could deliver in the industrial age. Indeed, it is the blockchain mindset and technology that enable industrial chain groups to lower transaction costs associated with information acquisition and establish more stable organizational structures, thereby fostering symbiosis and sharing.

Case Study: How the Six-sector Industrialization of Agriculture Can Contribute to "San Nong"?

Professor Zhang Laiwu, the founder of the Six-sector Theory, worked at the People's Government of Ningxia Hui Autonomous Region for 10 years. Back then, Ningxia was distinguished by its extensive mountains and deep valleys, a dry climate with minimal rainfall, ecological fragility, underdeveloped transportation infrastructure, isolated information systems, and technological backwardness. In 1972, the Food and Agriculture Organization of the United Nations classified the Xi-Hai-Gu area of Ningxia as one of the most inhospitable areas on the planet, dubbing it an "agricultural no-go zone".

Against such an ecological backdrop, Ningxia has managed to develop a wine grape industry that rivals those of world-renowned wine-producing areas, earning the moniker "Blue Miracle". This achievement stems from Ningxia's ongoing commitment to eco-agriculture exploration and practices. While Ningxia is still in the process of developing an eco-agriculture model tailored for the

digital era, it has already accumulated some proven experience. From the perspectives of ecology, data, and technology, I will now describe the journey of Ningxia's wine grape industry towards an eco-agriculture model.

First, Ningxia's natural conditions necessitate a green transformation to recalibrate the relationship between humans and nature. Confronted with acute water shortages and the aftermath of deserted mining endeavors, Ningxia could not pursue the path of US-style agricultural modernization. Instead, Ningxia's agricultural and industrial pathways are shaped by its natural resource endowment and the necessity of water conservation. Ningxia has initiated ecological restoration efforts along the eastern foothills of the Helan Mountains, repurposing former mining sites into vineyards covering over 10000 mu. With a wine grape cultivation area of 580000 mu (or 38860 hectares), these foothills stand as China's largest contiguous region for wine grape production. Thanks to the comprehensive governance of mountains, waters, forests, farmlands, lakes, grasslands, and deserts, 350000 mu (or 23450 hectares) of once barren terrain have turned into expansive oases, forming a green ecological barrier along the eastern foothills of the Helan Mountains. This achievement is made possible by the top-level design of the governments, the contributions and innovations of entrepreneurs from Fujian Province through the East-West collaboration mechanism, and the painstaking efforts of the residents.

Second, Ningxia must reduce production and transaction

costs through digital transformation. In 2008, Ningxia emerged as a pioneering region in rural informatization by launching a comprehensive farmer training program. This program aimed to nurture a number of IT-savvy farmers, propelling the informatization of "new countryside" across Ningxia. The approaches included "strong leadership, collaborative efforts, win-win innovation, multifaceted functions, online platforms, service extension, integrated resources, customized offerings, diverse funding sources, and long-term mechanisms". Starting with the selenium sand melon and goji berry bases in Zhongwei City, Ningxia's rural informatization initiative saw the establishment of an information service station in each of its 2362 administrative villages, creating a widespread network. Ningxia also built a centralized IPTV platform and a dedicated e-commerce platform, both underpinned by extensive data mining efforts. These platforms, along with Internet terminals, formed a comprehensive service framework for rural informatization. The framework's primary functions included providing online and call center support for technical issues, connecting farmers with larger markets for buying and selling, and facilitating cultural exchanges. The tripartite functions of Internet-based operations, cultural sharing, and training served to integrate online services across all aspects of rural life, leveraging every information service station for multiple purposes and extending its reach. Through the integration of various resources—informational, platform, network, organizational, financial, and social—Ningxia's rural informatization initiative

Six-sector Industrialization of Agriculture: TTF's Innovation and Entrepreneurship in the New Era

created an extensive, constantly updated, and valuable database, laying the foundation for subsequent development of the selenium sand melon, goji berry, Tan sheep, and wine grape industries.

Last but not least, Ningxia's rural industries have leveraged technological factors. The system of TTF, which is integral to an innovation and entrepreneurship model where both benefits and risks are shared with farmers, addresses the shortcomings in the government's agricultural technology outreach services. The TTF harnesses its know-how to create business ecosystems in collaboration with farmers and cooperatives, among other agricultural stakeholders. The core of these ecosystems lies in the utilization of each participant's strengths to amalgamate resources, develop new business models, and distribute the added value. This model differs both from the unilateral, top-down provision of public services by government technology extension departments and from the one-off transactions between farmers and suppliers of agricultural machinery or fertilizers. It encapsulates the eco-agricultural ethos of cooperation and sharing.

The preceding discussion offers a conceptual overview of the three pillars of eco-agriculture: ecology, data, and technology. Now, taking Ningxia's wine grape industry as an example, we will conduct a case study on the implementation of eco-agriculture models.

First, despite its focus on ecology, data, and technology,

Ningxia's wine grape industry also embraces the advancements ushered in by industrialization. Major wineries across the region have leveraged modern biotechnology and industrial processes, including the integration of advanced fermentation methods and sophisticated French winemaking practices into their industry chains. Furthermore, the selection of winery locations, along with the design of visitor routes, exhibitions, and recreational activities, demonstrates meticulous attention to detail. These efforts aim to enrich the tourist experience, while also ensuring that the product value resonates deeply with the human-centric philosophy ingrained in eco-agriculture.

Second, Ningxia's wine grape industry follows the path of integrated development. The industry aligns with the rural revitalization strategy by synergizing the primary (grape cultivation in contiguous areas), secondary (advanced wine-making techniques of modern industrial enterprises), and tertiary (wine tourism, wineries, and homestays) sectors. This approach, which breathes new life into the eastern foothills of the Helan Mountains, fosters the integrated development of grape farming, wine production, cultural tourism, and wellness businesses. It marks a significant departure from the traditional winery operation mindset, which viewed tourism as just a supplement.

Third, Ningxia's wine grape industry has fostered an expansive business ecosystem. This ecosystem is composed of multiple eco-partners: the planting phase involves large-scale growers,

cooperatives, and grape bases; the production phase highlights industrial enterprises with advanced brewing techniques and equipment; the marketing phase features an array of creatively designed wineries. The result is a multifaceted cultural framework that includes an orchard culture represented by vast vineyards, a wine-making culture defined by sophisticated processes, equipment, and containers, a steward culture enriched by traditions of vintage sampling and ceremonies, and a cultural tourism system that captures the essence of the Silk Road and regional attractions. Driven by the digital economy, online marketing and live-streaming media have also become eco-partners of Ningxia's wine grape industry in recent years.

Holansoul Winery, for example, has planted 3000 mu (or 200 hectares) of wine grapes and 9000 mu (or 600 hectares) of trees within the Gobi Desert, along with restoring 6000 mu (or 400 hectares) of deserted mining areas. Ningxia's wine grape industry follows an eco-friendly path, ensuring it "does not encroach on food supplies for humans or compete for agricultural land meant for grains, while also emphasizing the efficient use of water resources". This approach lays the groundwork for creating first a business ecosystem and then a social ecosystem. Despite the ongoing need for innovation in factors, paradigms, mainstream values, and lifetime user experience, Ningxia's wine grape industry is well on track to bringing eco-agriculture into shape.

Q3: What is Future Agriculture?

The future of agriculture is a sustainable one. Previously, agricultural modernization in developed nations was marked by a heavy reliance on petrochemical energy to provide ongoing mechanical power and chemical inputs, including fertilizers, herbicides, and preservatives, thereby boosting agricultural productivity. In contrast, China looks beyond food security and follows a green path to agricultural development, with "carbon neutrality" as the foundation for its future agriculture. In the quest for carbon neutrality, breakthroughs in biotechnology are poised to reveal novel business models. Many regions that would become unsuitable for crop cultivation might be suitable for "carbon sequestration" projects. And the synergy between biotechnology and digital technology will not only give these projects a big boost but also create a virtual platform for managing "carbon indicators". Through the digitization and ecosystemization of agriculture, carbon indicators can be measured and turned into commodities and high-value-added products. Eco-agriculture is set to forge new industrial and business paradigms where ecological assets, bolstered by digital technology, can be transformed into tangible wealth for farmers, thus converting ecological value into economic benefits.

First, as I said, the future of agriculture is a sustainable one. This

is of utmost importance. We need to assess agriculture's impact on various aspects of people's health, including physical, mental, social, and ecological ones. The agricultural sector has shifted its focus from ensuring food safety to balancing multiple functions. Each phase of the agricultural cycle, encompassing crop breeding, planting, management, processing, storage, and logistics to the dining table, needs to embrace the ethos of green development by employing eco-friendly technologies. Such a process views agricultural progress from an ecosystem's perspective and works towards the harmonious coexistence between humans and nature. Furthermore, even as human society moves from an industrial to a digital age, the foundational role of agricultural civilization, traced in China back to the Flaming and Yellow Emperors, must remain undiminished. Neither the declining share of GDP nor the reduction in the agricultural labor force can weaken the profound societal function of agriculture.

Second, the future of agriculture is empowered by digital intelligence. Future agriculture evolves through the deep integration of advanced technologies in communication, AI, and biology with conventional farming techniques. This evolution is epitomized by the advancement in seeds. The synergies between biotechnology and AI make it possible to develop crop varieties (chip seeds) that are resistant to high salinity and alkalinity, thereby converting vast expanses of saline-alkali land in China into productive fields. This approach marks a significant departure from traditional methods focused on modifying saline-alkali soils—an area where extensive

experience has been accumulated, albeit with high investment costs and sustainability concerns. Future breakthroughs in crop breeding will unlock new opportunities in saline-alkali land agriculture. So far, the advancement in technologies has already turned intelligent greenhouse management, tailored logistics solutions for farm produce, and bespoke delivery services for meal kits into reality. Moving forward, the further development of AI will take personalization to the next level, including offering nutrition plans based on customer needs. Future agriculture is poised to promote healthier lifestyles and extend lifespans.

The greatest discovery of human genius is the perfect harmony between the order of nature and the order of the mind. Should this maxim be actualized in future economic and industrial paradigms, it would serve as the cornerstone of eco-industrial evolution. The pressing concern over climate change and sustainable development is pushing human society further down the path of eco-agriculture, and the key to the six-sector industrialization lies in digital transformation. This digitization of agriculture should ensure that eco-friendly produce meets not only the physical needs of people but their emotional well-being as well. Instead of merely harnessing the achievements of industrial civilizations, the six-sector industrialization should forge new civilizations and industrial patterns for the digital age. Future agriculture relies on digital and ecological designs to foster natural, business, and social ecosystems. By creating lifetime user value and organizational models for chain groups, the agricultural sector will be able to pivot from division of

labor and market competition to integration and sharing. The digital age provides new opportunities for China's smallholder farmers, propelling them towards modernized agriculture while narrowing the urban-rural gap. To sum up, the six-sector industrialization heralds a promising future, and eco-agriculture stands as a new sector where traditional farming and modern industries thrive together.

Chapter III Methods for Developing the Eco-agriculture Program Based on the Six-sector Theory

Q1: Why is It Necessary to Develop the Eco-agriculture Program Based on the Six-sector Theory?

After the establishment of the Institute for Six-Sector Economy at Northwest A&F University and Fudan University in 2016, we published the first monograph on the sixth sector in People's Publishing House, *Six-sector Theory and Innovation-Driven Development*, in 2018. This book received widespread attention from readers. Many entrepreneurs, particularly those in agriculture, showed keen interest in how to operate the sixth sector. From 2016 to 2018, the Six-sector Theory establishes a theoretical framework to promote eco-agriculture. Within this framework, we identified digitalization (the fourth sector) as the key to the six-sector industrialization of agriculture, while the top-tier design for the six-sector industrialization relies on cultural and creative outputs (the fifth sector). So, who are the designers? Our pioneering explorations include the establishment of a non-corporate organization named

the Six-Sector Economy Innovation Center, which is overseen by the Bureau of Science and Technology of Yangling Agricultural Hi-tech Industries Demonstration Zone. This way, we can be both theoretically and practically prepared to undertake societal planning.

Why, at this stage, do we propose to develop an eco-agriculture program? This involves three aspects as follows.

First, what distinguishes China's eco-agriculture? It is closely related to our country's TTF system. As we mentioned earlier, the Six-sector Theory draws on the practical experience in respect of this system as well as Japan's six-sector industrialization of agriculture. This theory also owes its existence to the deep integration of the digital economy with AI-driven creative design. Building upon more than two decades of success in implementing the Chinese TTF system, we launched a TTF program with the National Committee, aiming to apply the Six-sector Theory to the design of eco-agriculture models. In a departure from conventional approaches, our program requires adherence to the principles of natural ecosystems while fostering business and social ecosystems for the era of digital civilizations. In this context, the business ecosystem represents the fourth sector, or the data sector, while the social ecosystem represents the fifth sector, encompassing cultural, creative, and cutting-edge scientific industries. If the business and social ecosystems were neglected, the six-sector industrialization would be reduced into agricultural evolution through the tertiary sector, without accounting for the added value from cultural and

scientific contributions. This oversight would hinder the creation of a high-value-added, virtuous agricultural cycle.

Second, what strategic approaches and channels are necessary for eco-agriculture? The crux lies in the digital transformation of the entire agricultural sector. Six-sector industrialization would be impossible without digital technology platforms and the data sector as a whole, not to mention new industry models and added value in the realm of eco-agriculture. The designs aimed at bridging the data sector with eco-agriculture will be explored in our later discussion.

Third, who incubated our program? Top-tier planning and design are paramount for the Six-sector Theory. So, exactly who should undertake the planning? The most qualified entities to apply the Six-sector Theory are the Institutes for Six-Sector Economy of Northwest A&F University and Fudan University, as they are the global pioneers of the sixth sector and the cradle of relevant research. A significant innovation in the operational model for eco-agriculture is the collaboration between two institutes and non-corporate entities to launch a specialized program. We are gearing up to promote this program across the country, working hand in hand with the National Committee for the TTF program, alongside stakeholders from governments, society, industries, universities, and institutes. Our goal is to establish this program as a key initiative for rural revitalization and industrial invigoration. This effort is poised not only to bridge China's longstanding urban-rural divide but also to chart a new course for agriculture. Looking ahead, we hope that an increasing number of think tanks and business

planning organizations equipped with the Six-sector Theory will help us design the eco-agriculture sector to realize agricultural modernization with Chinese characteristics.

Q2: What is the Eco-agriculture Program Based on the Six-sector Theory?

China trailed in agricultural industrialization during the industrial era, with its total factor productivity in agriculture hovering around 60% currently, which was considerably lower than that seen in developed nations like the US and the Netherlands. That is to say, China's primary sector was barely able to thrive. How to bolster the primary sector, constantly increase farmers' incomes, and improve the rural environment remains a pressing concern. In response, our central government calls for integrated development of the primary, secondary, and tertiary sectors. It has also successfully enacted a number of supportive policies. This approach fundamentally stems from the Six-sector Theory. However, there is a widespread ambiguity surrounding this theory and its practical application, which has led to a rudimentary comprehension of how these three sectors interrelate. Due to the lack of theoretical foundation, numerous efforts labeled as targeting the sixth sector in fact merge certain aspects of the primary, secondary, and tertiary sectors. Such efforts fall short of encompassing the Six-sector Theory.

Earlier, Xinhua News Agency conducted an official interview with the Institute for Six-Sector Economy of Fudan University. Subsequently, they communicated the Six-sector Theory to the

central government and made a public announcement highlighting the rapid advancement of the sixth sector in countries like Japan, South Korea, Germany, and especially China. During the interview, I pointed out that Japan is at the international forefront of the sixth sector, whereas China is the pioneer of the Six-sector Theory. Then what distinguishes China's sixth sector from Japan's? We believe China and Japan are evenly matched in this arena, with each country holding three advantages.

China's advantages are as follows. First, China "owns" the Six-sector Theory. In contrast, Japan's concept of the sixth sector merely represents a breakthrough in agricultural economics under the framework of the tertiary sector, i.e. sharing the benefits of the secondary and tertiary sectors with farmers by introducing processing and services businesses to rural areas. Japan has not conceptualized the fourth and fifth sectors, let alone the sixth. Second, the digital landscape in China outpaces Japan's. Leading Internet platforms in China, like Alibaba, JD.com, Tencent, Pinduoduo, and Douyin, are all involved in the marketing of agricultural products, indicating the digital superiority of China's fourth sector. Third, China has launched the TTF system. We will expand on the subject later in a dedicated chapter. This system fosters entrepreneurial partnerships between urban tech companies/ professionals and rural communities based on shared risks and benefits. As a foundation for the Six-sector Theory, it promotes cooperation between urban entrepreneurs and farmers throughout the entire industry chain.

Japan's advantages include the following. First, mechanization. Japan surpasses China in terms of industrialization and mechanization, thanks largely to its world-class small and micro agricultural machinery and advanced facility agriculture. Second, agricultural cooperatives. The Japanese Agricultural Cooperatives help the rural community acquire the means of production and market their products; they also offer financial services such as credit and insurance to rural households. These cooperatives are instrumental in advancing the six-sector industrialization, promoting the integrated development of the primary, secondary, and tertiary sectors, and ensuring that farmers benefit from these developments. Third, widespread adoption. Legislated in 2008, the concept of the six-sector industrialization has been implemented in numerous rural areas across the country since the 21st century.

Obviously, China holds the key advantage, as the country has systematically developed and deepened the Six-sector Theory. This theory has been evolving alongside the digital economy. Just as industrialization theories took shape during the shift from agrarian to industrial societies, the Six-sector Theory emerged amid the transition from the industrial to the digital age. The report from Xinhua News Agency underscores the necessity to initiate an eco-agriculture program. First, the program prioritizes eco-agriculture planning to nurture thriving businesses and promote sustainable development. Second, this era presents a historic opportunity to advance and apply the Six-sector Theory. We cannot afford to miss it. During the industrial age, most economic theories originated

from developed countries like the US, the UK, Germany, and France. As the era of digital civilizations dawns, it behooves China to push such theories further. And our eco-agriculture program is gearing up to do just that! Drawing on the successful experience of Japan's six-sector industrialization and China's system of TTF, we will promote eco-agriculture with the data prowess of our world-leading fourth sector and the creative designs from our fifth sector.

Q3: How to Operate the Eco-agriculture Program Based on the Six-sector Theory?

According to the Six-sector Theory, the fourth sector fuses data industries and agriculture to cultivate a digital business ecosystem; the fifth sector enriches smart agriculture with cultural and creative elements to establish a social ecosystem; and the sixth sector shares the benefits of "agriculture +" industries with the whole society. Our focus here is on fostering data-driven agricultural innovation. Specifically, we will explore how to develop the fourth sector and promote its integration with agriculture.

(I) How to foster data-driven agricultural innovation

The National Bureau of Statistics of China has adopted the two principles of the Six-sector Theory. First, it acknowledges data as an essential element of production. Second, it agrees that the digital economy has emerged as the predominant economic paradigm, succeeding the agricultural and industrial economies. According to the Bureau's *Statistical Classification of the Digital Economy and its Core Industries* (2021), the digital economy is defined as a series

of economic activities that use data resources as the key factors of production, and are based on the modern information network as an important carrier, and effective use of ICT as an important driving force for efficiency improvement and optimization of the economic structure. Digital industries are divided into five categories: 01"digital product manufacturing", 02"services related to digital products", 03"digital technology application industries", 04"digitally driven industries", 05"those focused on enhancing efficiency through digital means". The "Digital China Strategy" is designed to capitalize on the opportunities of the digital economy and share in its dividends. Hence, we have reasons to believe that the data sector (i.e. the fourth sector) can be effectively integrated with various industries, and agriculture is no exception.

First, integrate the data sector with agriculture. While the fourth sector of the Six-sector Theory, known as the "Internet $\oplus$ " sector, encompasses both agricultural and non-agricultural activities, it can choose to prioritize agricultural services. This sector is currently evolving towards a data-driven model, marking a shift from platform-based economies to data-centric industries. Data transcends mere numbers; it is increasingly recognized as a critical element of production. The transformation of data into a productive asset involves a sequence of steps including rights confirmation, pricing, transactions, and applications. In China, numerous platform economies are adopting this model, relying heavily on Internet platforms for the collection, accumulation, and utilization of data. This reliance outlines the structure of the data sector, which

functions through four specialized (industrial) modules. The first module explores who will supply the computing power for the development of smart agriculture, and at what cost. The second module deals with the ability for rapid software iterations. The third module concentrates on the gathering of data and knowledge. The fourth module revolves around the synergies of social networks. These modules represent a significant departure from industrialization, which is defined by corporate boundaries; instead, the fourth sector focuses on cross-module collaboration across society. As the cornerstone of the fourth sector, such collaboration enables rational data sharing. If we can build any of these modules well, we stand a chance to cultivate ecosystems. If we can run any of them well, potential business partners from other industries across the primary, secondary, and tertiary sectors will gravitate towards us.

Second, tackle the issues concerning eco-agriculture. The Six-sector Economy Theory underscores the critical importance of fully integrating the eco-agriculture innovation chain. It strongly advises against managing each link of the supply chain independently, which is an industrialization mindset focusing on the division of labor and market competition. In the digital economy era, although supply chains are still necessary, success hinges on the full integration and holistic design of innovation chains. To have its own business and social ecosystems, the agricultural sector must rely on a new element—data. Data-driven ecosystems prioritize cooperation and sharing over individualistic pursuits. Eco-partners

should be encouraged to willingly contribute their resources and work towards mutual benefits. In terms of full integration, the first step is to bolster market value and sales capabilities. Contrary to the prevalent approach of leveraging technology for its own sake, we should cultivate a "six-sector industrialization mindset", focusing on uncovering sources of added value. For Li Ziqi, the true value lay not in the quilts per se, but in the narratives they encapsulated; it was about addressing emotional rather than mere material needs. The best tool to promote products that fulfill high-value-added requirements is We Media, not e-commerce, let alone the expensive traditional sales networks. Sales on We Media rely on creative designs, which necessitates a tight linkage between the fourth and fifth sectors. These designs must be reasonable and compelling enough to encourage consumers to pay for added value. In the new era, sales strategies should prioritize customer experience over the producer-centric approach. Building large sales teams to push non-customized products is an outdated strategy from the industrial age. Although maintaining a sales network is still important, the focus should shift towards utilizing We Media for marketing, which has proven to be remarkably effective. A prime example is Dong Yuhui's foray into agri-product sales. In this case, the value proposition is not merely the products themselves but the cultural and creative narrative provided by New Oriental Education & Technology Group, coupled with Dong's personal insights.

Third, address the disconnection within the entire industry chain. Where does this disconnection occur? One of the challenges facing

the fourth sector is the inability of Internet platforms and financial institutions to forge connections with farmers at the end of the supply chain. Why supply chain finance (e.g. banks) failed? The problem lies in the fact that warehouse data are hard to verify, with occurrences of stock claims unbacked by actual inventory. Some sellers temporarily secured bank funds under pretenses, leading to situations where either the promised goods were unavailable when needed, or the delivered goods differed from those agreed upon. The instability of contracts with farmers exacerbates this problem. The farmer who sells products to you this year may choose to sell them to someone else, or at a different price, next year. So how to address this man-made disconnect? Two approaches are available. First, organize farmers through agricultural cooperatives or other entities. Second, establish the agricultural IoT to enhance data reliability and lower transaction costs. The strength of Japan Agricultural Cooperatives lies in its ability to mobilize farmers. In contrast, the lack of organization among Chinese farmers introduces instability, hindering the development of cohesive industry chains. Our case studies in supply chain finance have revealed the problems Internet companies, such as JD.com and Pinduoduo, face in penetrating lower-tier markets due to the disconnect with farmers. Despite Pinduoduo's close interaction with farmers and significant efforts in agricultural e-commerce, it still faces challenges in establishing firm connections. The disorganized farming communities lead to the natural incompatibility of agricultural bases with Internet platforms. So what can we do? China's TTF system could be

instrumental in organizing farmers. So could the agricultural IoT. Currently, Huawei is seeking to forge smart links with major production zones via sensors. Integrating IoT into Ningxia's wine grape cultivation, for example, could further enhance the industry's performance. The merger of agriculture and the IoT is closely connected with the sharing of data from the primary sector. The pathway forward involves either empowering farmers to engage with these technologies, creating an IoT infrastructure tailored for agricultural needs, or pursuing both strategies concurrently.

(II) How to foster the fifth sector

China's digital economy is experiencing swift expansion, the China Academy of Information and Communications Technology released its Research Report on the Development of China's Digital Economy(2023), China's digital economy has already exceeded an impressive RMB 50 trillion. Our nation boasts the most extensive and advanced network infrastructure globally, alongside the world's leading computing infrastructure. That is to say, China is reaping the benefits of its fourth sector, and the next driver of growth and value creation will be the fifth sector. The widespread adoption of eco-agriculture requires a multitude of entrepreneurs—particularly those from cultural and creative industries—who are in tune with the ethos of the digital era. These entrepreneurs will blend digital technologies with natural ecosystems, agricultural civilization, rural culture, and ethnic traditions to conduct creative designs, opening new pathways for adding value within the agriculture sector. Dear readers, I hope you will become entrepreneurs yourselves. Even

professors can be entrepreneurial, as advocated by the central government. In this day and age, embracing digital technologies is crucial for anyone from business leaders to farmers. If you fail to contribute to China's rural revitalization amid the six-sector industrialization, what is the use of being a professor in agricultural economics? By "use" I do not mean industrial utility but your life's value. Given the four modules of specialized data industry platforms, you can focus on forging connections with these platforms and the cultural and creative industries. The key lies in leveraging these platforms to meticulously design the eco-agriculture landscape. Equally important is the integration of theory with practice, as theoretical knowledge can reduce the trial-and-error process and costs. The point is, creativity in this context transcends materialistic needs, aiming instead to fulfill emotional desires. In the realm of the metaverse, for example, real estate may not provide tangible enjoyment, yet it can command high prices if it embodies innovative ideas rooted in cultural and creative expression.

The Research Center for Rural Economy of the Ministry of Agriculture and Rural Affairs (MARA), in collaboration with Shining Stone Think Tank, has sponsored the Yinji Xiangcun Creative Design Competition as an important element of the Yinji Xiangcun cultural program. This program adheres to the national directives on rural revitalization. Its goal is to bolster rural development through cultural and societal endeavors, specifically by tapping into the power of nostalgia. The program includes building the archives, organizing themed tours, and implementing

Six-sector Industrialization of Agriculture: TTF's Innovation and Entrepreneurship in the New Era

cultural and creative initiatives. The competition, with the theme of "Unearthing Diverse Values Through Creative Design to Lead the Future of Rural Areas", invites designers to delve into, preserve, and innovate upon the heritage of traditional local cultures, thereby making rural areas more suitable for work and living, and enhancing the quality and efficiency of cultural, creative, and other industries. This seamlessly aligns with the Six-sector Theory. Furthermore, the competition fosters collaboration among stakeholders from governments, society, industries, and research. As a national think tank for rural revitalization, the MARA Research Center for Rural Economy ensures that the competition complies with the central government's rural revitalization strategy. Experts, scholars, think tanks, creative design teams, university teachers and students, and rural stakeholders have actively participated in the competition. Focusing on the central task of establishing China as an agricultural power, the competition highlights Chinese rural cultural values while promoting the deep integration of modern design concepts with traditional farming practices. It encourages creative designs tailored for villages, rural landscapes, public facilities, and agri-product packaging, aiming to provide substantial support for the development of villages that not only serve professional and residential purposes but are also visually appealing. It is also conducive to stimulating the rural economy and boosting local society.

The emergence of the fifth sector can be attributed to the unique conditions fostered by the digital age which, unlike the industrial

or agricultural ages, lays the foundation for "storytelling" through the digital industry model. More significantly, this era marks an advanced post-industrial material civilization. In contrast to the past, contemporary mainstream values are gradually leaning towards personal aspirations and emotions, as well as the quest for individual freedom and ideals. Such a transformation contributes to the added value of eco-agriculture. Many industries within the metaverse are high-value-added because they cater to people's non-material needs. The growing aspirations for cultural and emotional fulfillment across society have sped up the evolution of the supply of such needs. These days, new media have emerged as a main channel of communication and cultural dissemination. The rise of new media has accelerated the development of digital cultural and creative industries. Some exceptional traditional cultures, including farming and rural traditions, are being swiftly spread through new media platforms. Furthermore, the digital cultural and creative industries, through the provision of virtual ecological space services and entertainment, have broadened the range of online cultural offerings. The art and design domain has evolved as well, with digital art products enabling online rights verification, transactions, and exhibitions. These shifts in both demand and supply have established the fifth sector as a driver of rural revitalization.

Nowadays, virtual products are doing an amazing job of meeting people's emotional requirements, thus leading to a transformation in mainstream values. The evolving alignment between what consumers want and what is provided is set to bring the fifth

sector into shape. Through collaboration among stakeholders from governments, society, industries, and research—as exemplified by the Yinji Xiangcun Creative Design Competition—we firmly believe that the fifth sector will play a significant role in rural revitalization efforts with Chinese characteristics.

Q4: How to Boost the Eco-agriculture Program Based on the Six-sector Theory through Innovation?

(I) Perception of science

To discuss how to boost eco-agriculture through innovation, one must first understand what science is. Modern society's perception of science tends to be incomplete or somewhat skewed. What is science? Let's first explore "God's Formula" conceived by Euler.

What is God's Formula? It refers to Euler's assertion that the series "$1 + 2 + 3 + ...$" sums to "$-1/12$". On the surface, this statement seems to contradict basic reasoning. The principles of elementary arithmetic imply that the result should be infinite. How, then, could it possibly be $-1/12$? Regarded as one of the Top Four mathematicians in history, Euler's answer left everyone dumbfounded, earning the formula its divine moniker. Srinivasa Ramanujan later provided preliminary proof that $-1/12$ is correct. The Riemann zeta function also supports the conclusion. This is what science is meant to be.

Through God's Formula, let's explore the essence of science. What drives the development of science? What is the primary purpose of scientific innovation? The genesis of God's Formula

has absolutely nothing to do with material or technological considerations. The true driving force behind scientific development is the mode of human existence. People might question the value of studying God's Formula, yet Euler utilized it to create a multitude of wonders. What appears to be useless may embody the essence of science.

Science is fundamentally about human existence. Contrary to the earlier view that science was purely technological or materialistic, it is now understood as an enabler for our way of life. This shift in perception leads to questions about the origins of science. Science originated exclusively from ancient Greece. Science and technology evolved on different paths until the 19th century when they began to merge. In modern times, China started learning Western science. What is the essence of Western science? As Albert Einstein put it, "The development of Western science is based on two great achievements: the invention of the formal logical system (in Euclidean geometry) by the Greek philosophers, and the discovery of the possibility to find out causal relationships by systematic experiment (during the Renaissance)". The logical system, as seen in Euclidean geometry, emerged from philosophical inquiry, not technological advancement, and is deeply imbued with cultural significance.

Building on these two great achievements, the Six-sector Theory introduces a new foundation for science in the digital age: artificial intelligence. AI transforms the landscape of scientific inquiry, which is moving away from traditional causality analysis toward correlation study. This signifies the advent of a new scientific

paradigm. Scientific endeavor ought not to be purely utilitarian; rather, it should embody the spirit of controversy, freedom, curiosity, and unyielding enthusiasm. This ethos mirrors that of Euler, who seemed predestined to conceive God's Formula. Sounds crazy, right? That is science.

Back to China. The national crisis we faced since the 19th century prompted us to embrace Western science for survival. This shift coincided with a transformative period in science characterized by its technologization, specialization, professionalization, and empowerment. Given our national circumstances, the coincidence has led to misconceptions about science's essence among the population. Many prioritize the development of technology while neglecting the scientific principles it is built upon, thus distancing our society from science's humanistic core. Our educational framework, particularly in terms of engineering disciplines, tends to focus on problem-solving and experimentation, without paying much attention to the historical, philosophical, and sociological dimensions of science. This has led to a divergence from the intended path in our societal values, scientific endeavors, and educational practices. The technologization, specialization, professionalization, and empowerment of Western science have also played a role in shaping China's current state, especially within military and industrial realms. Nonetheless, the digital era presents us with a fresh historical opportunity to recalibrate our perception of science and harness our collective intellect to adapt and thrive.

The power of technologization and professionalization stems

from the accelerated pace of innovation, which is also closely linked with digitization. Leveraging the rapid pace of industrialization and innovation, digitization showcases industrial prowess, military capabilities, and technological progress grounded in scientific advancements. Nonetheless, the traditional model of innovation is now deemed outdated. In the digital era, scientific insights can skip over technological processes to be directly utilized in production. That is where the triple helix model of innovation, which integrates science, technology, and market dynamics, comes in. Under this model, science alone can spawn services, eliminating the necessity for technological application. A case in point is AlphaGo, which has revolutionized people's understanding of the game of Go by digitizing millennia of human knowledge in merely three days. As a member of the AI family, AlphaGo owes its competitiveness and success to association study. When it comes to science-based innovation, we should first understand what science is, and why science and technology need to be independent yet intertwined. Science does not preclude technology; in fact, some technologies have their roots in scientific discoveries. However, it was not until the 19th century that technological inventions and scientific discoveries became interrelated. At present, science is closely tied to data. It leans heavily on knowledge and creativity and occasionally circumvents technological application. AI's continued development presents a significant opportunity for scientific innovation, especially in the realm of services. To sum up, we should not only rely on technology but also help science flourish.

(II) Innovation under the triple helix model

In the context of the triple helix model, it is critical to understand the impact of science-driven innovation, particularly in our data-centric era. The idea that science-driven innovation can meet the collective longing for shared emotional experience makes perfect sense. While the production of industrial goods may face technical hurdles, the metaverse offers a realm where scientific breakthroughs can be realized instantly without technological constraints. This is not to undermine technologies' importance but to highlight how science can directly inform the development of future services. I find the concept of the metaverse acceptable. However, from the perspective of the Sixth-sector Economy Theory, I beg to differ on certain widely accepted notions about the metaverse. Those who enthusiastically promote the metaverse often do so with the belief that virtual markets within it bypass the need for technology or the constraints of industrialization. They also argue that in the digital realm, the force of innovation constantly creates business opportunities and enriches scientific understanding, which in turn fosters new ways of living and new forms of social organization. The term "metaverse" originated from the American sci-fi novel Snow Crash by Neal Stephenson. The market enthusiasm surrounding the metaverse is partially due to the freshness of its concept which, when introduced to China, was embraced with a fervor similar to religious zeal. Although the metaverse's capacity for innovation is undeniable, the current comprehension of it remains lacking.

The metaverse carves out a separate realm parallel to our

physical existence, which is quite unnecessary. The Sixth-sector Economy Theory suggests that humanity lives within a single universe that transcends time and space. The metaverse is simply a facet of the digital era. Thus, the perception of the universe being bifurcated is a construct confined to scientific discourse. As the sixth sector fully embraces the digital age, the notion of parallel universes has become obsolete. This perspective challenges the metaverse's distinctiveness and rigidity as a concept.

Science gives wings to our imagination, offering us a lifestyle of unmatched grandeur. Embracing science is like a rebirth, a second chance to live life to the full. If God's Formula can be conceived by human minds, what limits could there possibly be to our imagination? The triple helix model of innovation ensures that scientific discoveries can swiftly reach the market, undeterred by the lack of patents. Operating within the metaverse does not require extensive business knowledge. The world is replete with marvels, moving beyond the confines of industrial societies to a place where the physical and the spiritual merge, and where the power of industrialization and the potential of digitization coexist.

From this perspective, the pivotal elements for advancing eco-agriculture are biotechnology and security technology. Let's take a look at symbiotic farming to illustrate. Unlike traditional farming practices, which tend to coddle crops through the use of pesticides, fertilizers, and substantial investments in labor and machinery, all in pursuit of higher yields and superior quality for a premium market price, symbiotic farming leans into the natural traits of

various plants that emerged from the fusion of biotechnology with digital technology. By cultivating these plants at varying heights, it creates the optimal conditions for natural growth. Likewise, people usually hold wild plants in higher regard, which are akin to those cultivated using symbiotic farming technologies. These technologies are the be-all and end-all of our eco-agricultural designs. Domestically, our efforts are supported by advanced technologies from new-countryside research institutes affiliated with 39 universities nationwide. The joint endeavors of these institutes ensure our agricultural methods are not only viable but also more environmentally friendly. Furthermore, enterprises across China are spearheading the establishment of eco-agriculture bases that capitalize on biotechnology and digital technology.

(III) Eco-agriculture bases

We place a particular emphasis on the construction of production bases for traditional Chinese medicinal materials, given their undeniable significance to human life and health. These bases need to be both eco-friendly and digitally empowered. Notably, China's "daodi" medicinal materials span across 15 key production areas, including Yunnan, Sichuan, and Tibet. Yet daodi medicinal cultivation is facing challenges due to soil and water contamination. To ensure the safety of daodi medicinal materials, the TCM industry must modernize through the six-sector industrialization. So how to make up the costs? The added value of digitally empowered daodi medicinal materials may come from two sources: enhanced quality and safety, and cultural and creative contributions (the fifth

sector). Thus, we will first explore the six-sector industrialization of traditional Chinese medicinal materials, hoping that pharmaceutical companies and cultivation sites will jointly develop the production bases concerned.

Equally important is carbon farming. Issued in August 2021, the 14th Five-Year National Plan for Green Agricultural Development defines the "accelerated construction of a low-carbon, circular agricultural system" as a pillar in the agriculture sector's pursuit of the "dual carbon" strategy. Issued in September 2021, the Opinions of the CPC Central Committee and the State Council on Completely, Accurately, and Comprehensively Implementing the New Development Concept and Ensuring Peak Carbon Dioxide Emissions and Carbon Neutrality place requirements on "improving carbon sequestration and efficiency in agriculture" and "increasing the carbon sink capacity of eco-agriculture". Under the "dual carbon" strategy, the significance of carbon farming cannot be overstated. The question is, where should the carbon farming bases be built? In October 2021, during an inspection of the saline-alkali land of the Yellow River Delta in Shandong, President Xi Jinping visited the modern agricultural experimental demonstration base. There, he observed various crops' growth and learned about the progress of preserving and comprehensively utilizing saline-alkali soils and promoting salt-tolerant crop varieties. He highlighted the strategic importance of such land to national food security.[1]

---

[1] 习近平:《论"三农"工作》，中央文献出版社，2022，第130页。

Salt-tolerant crops had already been cultivated locally during my service at the Ministry of Science and Technology. However, focusing exclusively on the primary sector is financially unviable. For example, Binzhou City in Shandong Province is exploring the strategy of a protective forest system that merges belts, nets, and patches. This system integrates farmland, roadway, and waterway forest networks to effectively reduce wind speed, which has been shown to boost crop yields by 10%. Binzhou's exploration spans from breeding to windbreak and sand fixation, yet the issue of exorbitant costs persists.

In May 2023, Binzhou launched Shandong's first voluntary greenhouse gas emissions reduction project targeting rural areas and agricultural practices. The project also occupies a leading position nationally. Why is that? Because the project adopts a dual-income model; it generates primary income through wheat harvesting and secondary income through carbon trading. If Binzhou leverages its extensive saline-alkali land to establish a six-sector industrialization base, it would contribute to the nationwide effort to retaining 1.8 billion mu (approximately 120.6 million hectares) of farmland. This is but one example of the benefits of developing eco-agriculture on saline-alkali soils.

Another case in point is the development of the six-sector industrialization base for wine grapes. As this topic was discussed in Chapter II, further repetition will be avoided here. First, we will focus on promoting the construction of eco-agriculture bases and devising implementation strategies for the six-sector

industrialization. When conditions are ripe, we will gradually expand these efforts beyond the realm of eco-agriculture.

Q5: What is the Organizational Model for the Eco-agriculture Program Based on the Six-sector Theory?

To conclude this chapter, let's discuss why and how eco-agriculture design should be coordinated through the National Committee for the TTF Program. Eco-agriculture design relies on collaboration among stakeholders from governments, society, industries, and research. While the concepts of industry-university-research collaboration and government-industry-university-researc partnership are well-established, social stakeholders are still new to this game. In this context, "government" does not mean government bodies. Instead, it encompasses directives and policies of the CPC Central Committee and the State Council regarding the comprehensive implementation of the rural revitalization strategy.

(I) Innovation through collaboration among stakeholders from governments, society, industries, and research

According to the Global Competitiveness Report 2019, China was ranked 28th worldwide in its ability to foster collaborative innovation between businesses, universities, and institutes. This places us far behind not only developed countries like the US, Japan, Germany, and the Netherlands but also Singapore and the Hong Kong SAR. In China, industry-university-researc innovation partnerships have an average lifespan of about three years, with

nearly half ending in failure. The original model of integrating governments, businesses, and institutes faced multiple operational challenges, including corruption and ethical dilemmas, which led to unsustainable practices during its widespread adoption. The root cause was the model's emphasis on division of labor and market competition, characteristic of the industrial era. In contrast, the principles of the six-sector industrialization are connection and integration among eco-partners based on mechanisms for consensus building and sharing. Relevant approaches include employing blockchain technology to secure eco-partners' information against unauthorized alterations and developing social ecosystems to earn eco-partners' trust. Building social ecosystems requires certain organizational behaviors. Within the realm of eco-agriculture, such behaviors entail harnessing the power of civic societies in the design of eco-agricultural initiatives.

What I mean by saying the "government" here does not refer to government bodies is that the government should not be seen as a direct partner in eco-agriculture design. Rather, such design should conform to the directives and policies of the CPC Central Committee and the State Council regarding rural revitalization, "digital China", and eco-civilization. The "Silicon Valley model" of the 1950s, epitomized by Stanford University, demonstrated a partnership between industries and research. As a novel organizational model, the collaboration among stakeholders from governments, society, industries, and research primarily aims to enhance the stability of collaboration networks. By allowing social

stakeholders to lead the design of the eco-agriculture program, we can garner widespread consensus and create a favorable environment for all partners, thereby fostering mechanisms for win-win cooperation and sharing. However, multi-party collaboration carries the risk of betrayal, thereby amplifying transaction costs and potentially undermining the sustainability of the partnership. The core solution, as we mentioned earlier, is to organize farmers, establish the agricultural IoT, and employ blockchain technology to ensure data integrity, thereby developing reliable trust-building mechanisms.

In the early stages of the six-sector industrialization, commercial consulting firms were not yet equipped with the Six-sector Theory. For businesses unable to undertake eco-agriculture design on their own, a practical alternative is to engage non-corporate organizations or those endorsed by the government, such as the National Committee for the TTF Program affiliated with the China Soft Science Research Association. Given its status as a social organization without commercial motives, the committee is well-positioned to offer eco-agriculture design services under the guidance of the Six-sector Theory, thanks to its collaboration with 39 new-countryside research institutes across the country. Additionally, it can drum up support from one million sci-tech experts sent to rural areas to promote eco-agriculture.

(II) The establishment of ecosystems for the six-sector industrialization
How should we establish eco-agriculture bases, with the National Committee for the TTF Program as the overarching planner and a million sci-tech experts as our supporters? We believe the triple

helix model of innovation can help us establish natural, business, and social ecosystems, thereby promoting the construction of eco-agriculture bases.

First, identify potential technology collaborators for the development of natural ecosystems. Earlier, we talked about carbon farming in Binzhou. Carbon farming requires not only low-carbon agricultural technologies but also digital and carbon trading technologies. According to the information from the Department of Ecology and Environment of Fujian Province, the bamboo management and carbon sequestration project at Changting Louziba Forest Farm, along with the forest management and carbon sequestration projects at Wuyishan Experimental Forest Farm and Jianning County Forestry Construction Investment Company, have been registered and sanctioned by the Fujian Province's Department of Ecology Environment (Provincial Carbon Trading Office). These three projects span 11000 hectares and achieved a carbon sequestration tally of 329000 tons during the first monitoring phase. Since 2016, Fujian has been at the forefront of the nation, trading 2.839 million tons of forestry carbon credits valued at RMB 41.829 million. This highlights the role of forestry carbon sequestration in converting ecological value into economic benefits. These successful regional practices play a crucial role in the advancement of eco-agriculture. In another example, the "Juncao" technology, pioneered by Professor Lin Zhanxi of Fujian Agriculture and Forestry University, has not only propelled a significant eco-agricultural initiative within the Fujian-Ningxia collaboration

framework but has also gained traction in numerous developing countries across Africa and Latin America.

Second, build business ecosystems for agriculture. Here, the term "business ecosystem" is used within the context of the Six-sector Theory. To build such an ecosystem, it is essential to forge partnerships with platform companies from the fourth sector and with creative designers from the fifth sector. Financial resources can be secured through rural revitalization funds set up by these platform companies or through their own ESG and commercial investments. As for the fifth sector, organizations like the Yangling Sixth-Sector Economy Research Center, the National Committee for the TTF Program, and the Alliance of New-Countryside Research Institutes have the potential to become eco-planners. Furthermore, the million-strong TTF can be directly involved in the execution of eco-agriculture projects.

Third, establish social ecosystems for agriculture. The term "social ecosystem" as used here denotes a society-wide consensus that a digital civilization should cater to people's emotional needs—such as their nostalgic affections, aspirations, ideals, and a connection to nature. This consensus emphasizes the digital mindset behind thriving rural businesses, as opposed to the conventional industrial mentality. It promotes the widespread recognition of the equal significance of virtual domains, such as the metaverse, alongside the physical realm. This perspective, reminiscent of "God's Formula", enables individuals to perceive reality through a multi-dimensional lens. By cultivating such a collective mindset, society progresses towards the attainment

Six-sector Industrialization of Agriculture: TTF's Innovation and Entrepreneurship in the New Era

of the SDGs. This departure from unchecked material pursuits contributes to enhancing people's emotional well-being, facilitated by the application of science, AI, wisdom, and creative design. The integration of these components with San Nong transcends the urban-rural dichotomy, thus opening up new avenues for rural revitalization.

What kind of agriculture do natural, business, and social ecosystems represent? Future agriculture. Future agriculture will seamlessly integrate with nature while promoting the harmonious coexistence between urban and rural communities. This type of agriculture is both forward-looking and sustainable. The China Future Industry Index, recently released by Tencent Research Institute, covers several fields with future relevance: information, ecology, materials, manufacturing, energy, and space. The fusion of cutting-edge technologies from these fields, including biotechnology, AI, and communication technology, is expected to propel the evolution of agriculture towards a sustainable future.

Chapter IV   Innovation and Entrepreneurship of the Technical Task Force (TTF)

The TTF system stands out as a major institutional breakthrough, leveraging the expertise of Chinese sci-tech experts to bolster San Nong. This system has undergone three key stages. It was first launched in Nanping, Fujian in 1999, and subsequently promoted nationwide by the Ministry of Science and Technology, garnering widespread acclaim and success. In 2016, the system was integrated into the national policy agenda as the General Office of the State Council released the Opinions on Deepening the Implementation of the TTF System. In 2019, President Xi Jinping commemorated the system's 20th anniversary with an important directive, underscoring its essential role in driving rural rejuvenation through the deployment of innovative talent.[1] The enduring vitality of the TTF system hinges on its constant iteration and refinement in response to the six-sector industrialization of agriculture.

---

[1] 本书编写组编《闽山闽水物华新——习近平福建足迹（上）》，人民出版社、福建人民出版社，2022，第 320 页。

Q1: How Has the TTF System Evolved from Its Initial Pilot in Nanping to Widespread Adoption across China?

The TTF system originated in Nanping, Fujian. To address a range of San Nong issues, in 1998, over 3000 officials from Nanping were deployed to conduct field surveys in rural areas. It was in such a context that the TTF system was implemented in 1999. This system addressed the shortage of technological services available to rural communities by deploying officials with technological expertise to the agricultural front lines. These officials offered advice, training, and demonstrations while receiving their original compensation and benefits. In 2002, following a specialized investigation into this program, Xi Jinping, who was the Governor of Fujian Province at the time, shared his insights in an article for QIUSHI magazine. The article, titled "Striving for Innovation in Rural Work Mechanisms: An Investigation and Reflection on the Dispatch of Officials to Rural Areas in Nanping, Fujian Province", praised the program as a valuable innovation in rural work within the framework of a market economy, and recommended a thorough analysis of it.

In 2002, building on the "Nanping experience", the Ministry of Science and Technology decided to pilot the TTF system in western regions, including Ningxia. In response to the shortage and underqualification of local technological professionals, Ningxia implemented the system throughout its cities and counties, aiming to bolster rural industries and farmers' earnings based on a mechanism that leverages both governmental support and

market-driven services. These efforts gave rise to the Ningxia model, marked by a strong emphasis on fostering technological entrepreneurship.

In 2003, Zhejiang also piloted the TTF system, with the first batch of 101 sci-tech experts sent to 25 underdeveloped towns and townships across the province to carry out poverty alleviation operations. Xi Jinping, then Secretary of the Zhejiang Provincial Party Committee, issued an important directive on the system, identifying it as a proper innovative measure aimed at resolving technological difficulties in agricultural production and operations and training applicable skills.[①]

In 2004, the Ministry of Science and Technology and the former Ministry of Personnel issued the Opinions on Piloting the Grassroots Entrepreneurship Program for the Technical Task Force (Guo Ke Fa Zheng Zi [2004] No. 542), promoting the TTF system nationwide. This program introduced distinctive and innovative approaches in various aspects such as team building, service models, service functions, service channels, management systems, and theoretical exploration.

In 2006 and 2007, the Ministry of Science and Technology, the Ministry of Personnel, and the Ministry of Agriculture convened a pilot work meeting in Nanping, Fujian Province, and an experience exchange meeting in Liaocheng, Shandong Province, to further

---

① 本书编写组编《闽山闽水物华新——习近平福建足迹（上）》，人民出版社、福建人民出版社，2022，第318页。

Six-sector Industrialization of Agriculture: TTF's Innovation and Entrepreneurship in the New Era

promote the TTF system across the country. Additionally, the Ministry of Science and Technology, the Ministry of Commerce, and the United Nations Development Programme jointly launched a project, "Exploration of Innovative and Long-term Mechanisms for Technology-Driven Poverty Alleviation for China's Rural Areas". This paved the way for the vigorous development of technological entrepreneurship and innovation.

In 2009, the Ministry of Science and Technology, the Ministry of Human Resources and Social Security, the Ministry of Agriculture, the Ministry of Education, the Publicity Department of the CPC Central Committee, the State Forestry Administration, the Central Committee of the Communist Youth League, and the China Banking Regulatory Commission jointly established a coordination and steering group for the TTF's entrepreneurship in rural areas. The eight agencies also issued the Opinions on Deepening the Rural Entrepreneurship Program for the Technical Task Force (Guo Ke Fa Nong [2009] No. 242), held a national work conference for the TTF, and initiated the TTF rural entrepreneurship program. Subsequently, the State Forestry Administration, the All-China Federation of Supply and Marketing Cooperatives, the Central Committee of the Communist Youth League, and the All-China Women's Federation successively launched their industry-specific TTF entrepreneurship programs.

For five consecutive years from 2012 to 2016, TTF tasks were covered by China's No. 1 central document. In May 2016, the General Office of the State Council released the Opinions on

Deepening the Implementation of the TTF System (Guo Ban Fa 〔2016〕 No. 32). Following the issuance of these opinions, various regions and departments enhanced their organizational leadership, optimized work mechanisms, developed service platforms, increased publicity and guidance efforts, and heightened the enthusiasm of all involved parties. This not only further ignited the TTF's passion for innovation and entrepreneurship but also fostered the robust growth of relevant programs. Guided by these opinions, a million sci-tech experts are serving rural industries throughout China.

On October 21, 2019, a summary meeting on the 20-year-old TTF system was held in Beijing, where President Xi Jinping's important directives were conveyed. President Xi noted that over the past 20 years, the system has been committed to connecting the rural community with talent and technology. The ever-growing TTF has established itself as an advocate for the Party's San Nong policies, a conduit for spreading agricultural technologies, a front-runner in technological innovation and entrepreneurship, and a trailblazer in combating rural poverty. In so doing, the TTF has enhanced the sense of fulfillment and happiness among a large number of farmers.[①] President Xi underscored the vital role of innovation in driving the comprehensive revitalization of rural areas. He highlighted that the TTF system had a greater role to play in driving rural rejuvenation through the deployment of innovative

---

① 本书编写组编《闽山闽水物华新——习近平福建足迹（上）》，人民出版社、福建人民出版社，2022，第 320 页。

talent. He added that the sci-tech experts working in rural areas should remain true to their aspirations and continue to contribute towards poverty alleviation and rural revitalization.[①]

Q2: From Local Practices to a National Policy, How Does the TTF System Maintain Its Enduring Vitality?

From a developmental standpoint, the TTF system is not characterized by a rigid set of institutional arrangements. Instead, it represents a constantly evolving system of rural innovation and entrepreneurship. This system owes its enduring vitality to the synergistic interplay of theoretical, institutional, technological, and industrial innovations.

(I) From technological services to technological entrepreneurship

When the idea of the TTF was first introduced in Nanping, the pre-existing system for promoting agricultural technology, developed under the planned economy regime, was falling apart. It was, therefore, unable to satisfy the robust need of San Nong for technological services. Moreover, agricultural technology professionals were mainly working within institutional environments such as universities, research institutes, and agencies dedicated to the promotion of such technologies. These individuals were largely detached from front-line agricultural production. The "Nanping experience" utilized governmental policy frameworks to

---

① 本书编写组编《闽山闽水物华新——习近平福建足迹（上）》，人民出版社、福建人民出版社，2022，第 320 页。

motivate tech workers to move from institutional roles to market-oriented positions, thereby providing technological services that would aid in advancing the agricultural sector and rural communities. As the experience gathered momentum, tech workers forged "communities of shared interests" with rural enterprises, cooperatives, and village collectives, serving as major contributors to local industries.

In a slight departure from the "Nanping experience", the "Ningxia model" pioneered the TTF entrepreneurship scheme. Back then, Ningxia did not even have enough tech workers in institutional roles. In response, Ningxia opened the doors of the TTF to anyone possessing the technological acumen to propel rural industrial advancement, leveraging the innovative and entrepreneurial forces from "outside the institution" to serve San Nong. For instance, Ningxia facilitated collaborations between technology-driven agricultural enterprises and rural communities, fostering innovation at the grassroots level. Subsequently, the Ministry of Science and Technology promoted this model nationwide, and the State Council's No. 32 document of 2016 gave the spotlight to the TTF's innovation and entrepreneurship. In retrospect, the transition from providing technological services to promoting technological entrepreneurship represented not merely a tentative probe but a historic shift in the perception of innovation.

Under conventional industrial development paradigms, the journey of agricultural technology from inception to adoption by farmers was typically linear and long, encompassing lab research,

field tests, pilot launches, promotional efforts, and other stages. Cross-functional interaction was difficult as the stakeholders were scattered. Nonetheless, the advent of the Internet and the digital economy has created a cyclic momentum among science, technology, and the market, with science and technology evolving from primarily exogenous factors of production to primarily endogenous ones. Therefore, the technological service model based on the "linear innovation theory" is inevitably replaced by the "triple helix model of innovation"[1]. Despite witnessing the aftermath of the global Internet bubble, the year 2002 marked the onset of China's online economy boom. Given the Internet's transformative impact on traditional industries, the "Ningxia model" was crafted in line with the "Internet +" entrepreneurship scheme from the very beginning. The TTF encompasses not just those with institutional roles but also businesses and individuals that can meld modern production factors such as technology, information, talent, management, and capital into the agricultural and rural landscape. As a result, these stakeholders have turned from external contributors to internal catalysts of rural industrial growth. According to the Ministry of Science and Technology, By 2017, [2]Chinese sci-tech experts (individuals) sent to rural areas totaled 739000, serving around 65 million farmers. The TTF has significantly modernized and sophisticated China's agricultural

---

[1]　For more details about the triple helix model of innovation, please refer to 张来武:《科技创新的宏观管理：从公共管理走向公共治理》,《中国软科学》2012 年第 6 期。

[2]　《深入推进大众创业万众创新，全社会创新创业活动进一步激发》, https://www.most.gov.cn/ztzl/qgkjgzhy/2017/2017pd2016/201701/t20170110_130388.html。

sector while contributing immensely to the prosperity of rural communities. In the pursuit of innovation-driven development, technological entrepreneurship has successfully redefined technological services.

(II) From the introduction of factors to the cultivation of industry models

In 1964, Theodore W. Schultz, an American economist, published a book entitled "Transforming Traditional Agriculture". This book points out that incorporating new factors of production is a crucial means to revolutionize traditional agriculture, thereby increasing productivity and transforming agriculture into a catalyst for economic growth. In 1979, Schultz, along with Arthur Lewis—who is known for his dual sector model—was honored with the Nobel Prize in Economics. Governments and research have since broadened the application of Schultz's insights, and the infusion of modern production factors into traditional industries has become a fundamental strategy for industrial development. The success and ongoing evolution of the TTF's entrepreneurial efforts affirm the effectiveness of integrating modern elements. As President Xi Jinping has noted, the TTF stands at the forefront of technological innovation and entrepreneurship.[1]

However, as policymakers, we have to ask: How to incorporate modern elements into agriculture and rural areas? To find the answer, we must fully grasp the patterns and trends of rural

---

① 本书编写组编《闽山闽水物华新——习近平福建足迹（上）》，人民出版社、福建人民出版社，2022，第 320 页。

industrial development, given that the impact of modern elements differs across various industrial contexts. For instance, where conventional smallholder farming is concerned, the TTF is primarily engaged in introducing new agricultural varieties and technologies to farmers. Under traditional produce processing models, sci-tech experts become either full-time or part-time employees who aid rural companies in developing new technologies and products. However, in the Internet platform economy, these experts can ascend to corporate leadership roles, leveraging factors such as technology, information, capital, and labor to foster innovative development.

Based on our understanding of this issue, our approach to promoting TTF's entrepreneurship extends beyond simply introducing sci-tech experts as a modern element to rural areas. We also strive to incubate emerging and pioneering industries to enhance technological entrepreneurship and create job opportunities. In 2006, during my tenure as Vice Chairman of Ningxia Hui Autonomous Region, I spearheaded a rural informatization program in the region. This program aligned with the platform economy model, aiming to cultivate new industry models in rural areas. The pathway for rural informatization in Ningxia involved the government setting up a non-profit information service platform which, in turn, would encourage market players to develop commercial information service platforms in support of comprehensive rural informatization and technological entrepreneurship. Upon my transition to the Ministry

of Science and Technology in 2008, I facilitated the collaboration between our ministry, the Organization Department of the CCP, and the Ministry of Industry and Information Technology. Together, we launched a pilot project in 2010 to establish national rural informatization demonstration provinces[①]. Building on Ningxia's agricultural and rural informatization blueprint and following the principles of the Sixth-sector Economy Theory, we focused on "online platforms, service extension, and multifaceted functions" to foster an incubation platform for rural industries.

(III) From government-led to dual engine-driven

From a developmental standpoint, governments at various levels have actively supported the development, trial, and widespread implementation of the TTF system. The "Nanping model" attributes the system's creation to an "activist government". With the issuance of State Council Decree No. 32 of 2016, regions and departments across the country earnestly enacted the principles outlined in the document. They enhanced top-level planning, improved work mechanisms, developed service platforms with a people-centric mentality, intensified promotion to mobilize all stakeholders, and further sparked interest in innovation and entrepreneurship within the TTF. These efforts created a win-win scenario for the government and the market, bringing the TTF and farmers closer together. They also promoted the transformation and upgrade of agricultural industries and boosted rural communities, thereby

---

① For more details, please refer to 张来武等:《第四产业: 来自中国农村的探索》, 人民出版社, 2018。

facilitating the organic integration of institutional and technological innovation.

A significant reason for the TTF's success in driving rural industrial development through entrepreneurship lies in the government's consistent market-oriented approach. Being market-oriented means adhering to market principles. Over the past 20 years, China has seen a wave of sci-tech experts who, driven by selfless dedication, have offered farmers technological services at no cost. Many of these experts, through technological entrepreneurship, have realized shared prosperity for themselves, for farmers, and for the broader industries. Being market-oriented also involves creating opportunities for the TTF's entrepreneurship by establishing platforms and fostering favorable environments. Market-oriented institutional innovation boosts the economic performance of rural industries. Across China, the Six-sector Theory and other strategies have guided local piloting and demonstration, the construction of public platforms, experience sharing, and the shaping of public opinion. Therefore, the triumph of the TTF system signifies the successful shift from a government-led model to a dual engine-driven one.

As the TTF's entrepreneurship transitions from a macro policy to practices in specific fields, the government has a new role to play. During my time with the Ministry of Science and Technology, I advocated for the expansion of the TTF's entrepreneurship through societal engagement. Relying on the Collaborative Innovation Strategic Alliance of New-Countryside

Development Institutes affiliated with various universities, we inaugurated the "World of Entrepreneurs", an agricultural maker space. Furthermore, we started equipping the TTF with registered instead of designated members and establishing social entities like the TTF Alliance, aiming to foster autonomous growth within the TTF. These strategies and measures will remain relevant in the future. Theoretically speaking, a market-oriented approach might encounter "market failures", in which case an activist government is needed to rectify such issues. Similarly, a government-led model might encounter "government failures", in which case a well-functioning market is needed to take corrective actions. When failures in both domains coexist, social organizations need to come to the fore and provide emergency services. Therefore, the TTF's enduring vitality hinges on a collaborative framework involving government policies, market forces, and diverse social stakeholders.

Q3: What are the Main Models for the TTF?

(I) The Nanping model

The TTF system originated in Nanping. During his inspection visit to Fujian in March 2021, President Xi Jinping once again fully affirmed the TTF's work in Nanping City. In recent years, with President Xi's guidance, the TTF work mechanism of the Nanping model has incorporated new elements and developed platforms for exchanges and training. This evolution has injected fresh energy into rural revitalization efforts. Having been refined through

over two decades of practice, the Nanping model is now adopted in Fujian Province and across China. It presents the following characteristics:

First, the Nanping model has established an integrated TTF network. Under the comprehensive coordination of the municipal TTF leading group, TTF service centers, stations, and rooms have been established at the county, township, and village levels respectively. This structure has created a work mechanism characterized by "centralized management under principal officials and targeted oversight by designated leaders" alongside "interdepartmental collaboration and vertical integration".

Second, the Nanping model has developed new selection and deployment methods for the TTF. Nanping has transcended the traditional confines of specialization, identity, and location by expanding the TTF system. This expansion has seen the system evolve from supporting just the primary sector to encompassing secondary and tertiary sectors, from offering singular technological solutions to delivering a broad array of services, and from addressing the needs of specific segments to facilitating services across entire industry chains. As of March 2024, Nanping has 1985 individuals, 134 teams, and 7 organizations operating within this system. [①]The majority of these individuals were sci-tech experts, the teams usually consisted of research institutes offering collective services, and the organizations were partly made up of

---

① 《把论文写在田野大地上——南平市深入推进科技特派员制度三年工作综述》,《闽北日报》2024 年 3 月 24 日,第 1 版。

companies.

Third, the Nanping model has strengthened fintech support for innovation and entrepreneurship. Nanping has launched the "Ke Te Dai" program（Loan for TTF）, an innovative lending product aimed at supporting companies that are led, founded, or served by sci-tech experts sent to rural areas. In response, the municipal finance and the provincial agricultural financing guarantee company have jointly established a fund guarantee pool, and in collaboration with commercial banks, introduced the "Zheng Yin Dan" program, which translates to "government- and bank-guaranteed Ke Te Dai", aiming to foster a community of shared interests. Furthermore, Nanping has initiated the "Ke Te Mai" program to drive the sales of specialty produce through a digital platform.

(II) The Zhejiang model

On March 27, 2003, the General Offices of Zhejiang Provincial Government, following the important directives of Xi Jinping, then-Party Chief of Zhejiang, issued the Notice on Deploying Technical Task Force to Underdeveloped Towns and Townships and launched a technology-driven poverty alleviation program. The Zhejiang model, originally conceived for poverty alleviation, subsequently broadened its scope to encompass new-countryside construction, rural revitalization, ecological restoration, and "TTF for the industrial sector".

First, the Zhejiang model has targeted underdeveloped towns and townships since its inception, aiming to support them through the development of science and technology. In the critical

Six-sector Industrialization of Agriculture: TTF's Innovation and Entrepreneurship in the New Era

phase of poverty alleviation, the Zhejiang model evolved into a technology-driven precision partnership paradigm termed "1+N". This paradigm encompasses "1+N" technology service groups, promotional task forces, and local expert support teams under the TTF system. Zhejiang not only leverages the TTF for rural industrial support but also constantly enhances its own forestry and eco-technology service system for ecological preservation and restoration. Zhejiang is well on track to becoming a forest-rich province and is leading the charge towards technology-driven forestry modernization.

Second, the Zhejiang model has made positive explorations in refining government and market mechanisms. It has broadened the TTF talent pool through a collaborative approach involving governments, universities, institutes, companies, and rural teams. This approach has also enhanced the development of technology service organizations within towns and townships. On the other hand, the Zhejiang model harnesses the market's role in distributing technological resources to boost the TTF program. This in turn incentivizes TTF working in rural areas to promote new varieties, technologies, and products, develop industrial projects with significant impact, foster local growth points, and increase farmers' incomes.

In conclusion, Zhejiang has combined government and market forces to establish a market-oriented, technology-driven, government-led TTF work mechanism with both risks and interests shared with farmers. This mechanism underpins the vitality of the

TTF system.

(III) The Ningxia model

The Ningxia model is characterized by the TTF's innovation and entrepreneurship. As legal entities provide fertile soil for innovation and entrepreneurship, they constitute more than half of the TTF members in Ningxia. At the heart of the Ningxia model lies innovation and entrepreneurship. In Ningxia, the TTF's vitality is attributed not only to the guidance from the government but also to the momentum generated by innovation, entrepreneurship, and digitization amid the rural revitalization efforts. Beyond innovation and entrepreneurship, the Ningxia model presents the following characteristics.

First, the Ningxia model treats information as a new factor of production to enhance agricultural efficiency. The model, since its inception, has recognized "information" as a new production factor. It embraces the "online platforms + service expansion" approach to drive informatization. The push towards rural informatization has infused the TTF's innovation and entrepreneurship with fresh dynamism.

Second, the Ningxia model promotes the delivery of collective services via TTF consortia. Aiming for the integrated advancement of county-specific industries, Ningxia facilitates the establishment of TTF consortia to offer collective services in rural areas.

Third, the Ningxia model upholds the TTF spirit of East-West collaboration. Given the limited technological manpower in Ningxia, Professor Lin Zhanxi from Fujian has spearheaded

a pioneering initiative where TTF from China's more developed Eastern regions bring their experience and expertise to the West in support of local poverty alleviation and rural rejuvenation efforts. Such an initiative underscores the strengths of China's political institution.

So far, we have briefly introduced three TTF models, but this is just the tip of the iceberg. In fact, a wide variety of TTF programs are thriving across China, which ushers in a new era of TTF innovation and entrepreneurship.

Q4: What Challenges Does the TTF Face in the Comprehensive Promotion of Rural Revitalization?

Currently, the TTF is encountering some difficulties in its innovation and entrepreneurship efforts. The reasons, I believe, are two-fold. First, the external environment for the TTF's entrepreneurship has changed. The year 2023 was marked by post-pandemic economic recovery and development. The Central Economic Work Conference has underscored the problems and challenges impeding the economy's further recovery. These include the lack of effective demand, capacity surplus in specific industries, weak social expectations, and a plethora of risks. Moreover, there are evident constraints within the domestic cycle, let alone the growing bleakness, complexity, and uncertainty of the international landscape. In light of these conditions, it is small wonder that the TTF is facing difficulties with entrepreneurship.

Yet it is unfair to attribute the situation solely to external

factors. In fact, since 2020, the digital economy has witnessed robust growth, fueled by the accelerated advancement of industry digitalization and digital industrialization. Emerging technologies such as blockchain, VR, AI, and the metaverse have all achieved revolutionary breakthroughs. The primary reasons for the TTF system's current stagnation are internal, including the delay in grasping the rural industrial trends, lack of theoretical innovation, inadequate exploration of development pathways, and untimely formulation of effective policies.

Thus far, a million TTFs in rural China have engaged in technological entrepreneurship. The challenge lies in keeping them organized. There are currently no TTF organizations at the national level; nor are there any digital platforms catering to the TTF. However, on the provincial and municipal levels, some TTF management platforms are notably dynamic. For instance, Nanping's TTF cloud platform has integrated features such as information management, AI diagnostics, and the visualization of technological accomplishments.

In conclusion, the current standstill in TTF's entrepreneurial ventures presents both challenges and opportunities. As Zhejiang marked the 20th anniversary of the TTF system in 2023, President Xi Jinping's reply to local TTF representatives highlighted the importance that the national government attaches to the system. Although the TTF has seen an improvement in its online sales abilities thanks to previous practices, the requirements of the fourth sector surpass these advancements in the digital age. On

one hand, the advent of cutting-edge technologies like AI, 5G, AGI, and cloud computing introduces new hurdles for the TTF in terms of technology selection and application. On the other hand, as consumer preferences shift from uniform material goods to non-material rural offerings, embracing agriculture's multifaceted roles and rural areas' diverse values, alongside fostering growth in consumption through creative design, will serve as a new driving force for the TTF's entrepreneurship.

Chapter V   Building the Fourth Sector through the Technical Task Force (TTF)

Q1: What is the Current State of the Fourth Sector in Rural China?

Since the 1990s, data has emerged as a crucial driver in the new round of technological revolution and industrial transformation. Due to national policy support, rural information infrastructure, IT innovations and applications, and the fourth sector's recognition of data as a key production factor have played increasingly important roles in rural economic and social activities.

First, let's talk about the fourth sector's exploration and practice in rural areas. Since the 18th CPC National Congress, the Party and the government have vigorously implemented the strategy of transforming China into a cyberpower as well as the "Internet +" action plan. These efforts have catalyzed the comprehensive digitization of the socioeconomic landscape. Supported by national policies, the fourth sector has intensified its efforts in rural exploration and practice, positioning itself as a pivotal force

in resolving the San Nong issues in the digital era. Across China, innovative practices tailored to local needs have marked significant progress in devising the paths and methods for rural advancement of the fourth sector.

In 2006, Ningxia embraced Internet platform thinking to propel the growth of its fourth sector through five approaches: online platforms, service extension, tri-networks integration, long-term operations, and all-win innovation. First, online platforms: Ningxia established comprehensive rural information service platforms across the region, creating an agricultural information database to enhance the utilization efficiency of information resources. This approach allows for the accumulation of extensive service data and unimpeded information sharing. Second, service extension: Leveraging the region's central platform, Ningxia developed an IPTV sub-platform that delivers Internet video services, such as live TV, TSoC, and on-demand culinary content, to 20000 rural inhabitants. Information service stations, regarded as crucial to the digital transformation of the new countryside, were established in accordance with the "five ones" criteria: a permanent location, a suite of information equipment, an information officer, a set of management guidelines, and a long-term mechanism with assessment measures. Third, three-networks integration: to address the challenge of fragmented network resources, Ningxia integrated the telecommunications networks, cable TV networks, and the Internet, with IPTV serving as the gateway for this merge. Fourth, long-term operations: the introduction of the TTF system

marked a significant exploration into the "public services + corporate operations" mechanism that balances the interests of the government, rural households, and social stakeholders. This mechanism promotes market-oriented digital transformation of the new countryside while serving San Nong. Fifth, innovation and win-win cooperation: Ningxia fostered an environment where various stakeholders could benefit from cost-effective digitalization.

In 2020, the Ministry of Science and Technology, in collaboration with the Organization Department of the CPC, the Ministry of Industry and Information Technology, and the Cyberspace Administration of China, initiated the construction of national model provinces for rural informatization. Following the guidelines of "online platform, service extension, resource integration, and multifaceted functions", Shandong utilized its provincial Party member distance education network to pioneer the "1+N" service model that blends public services with commercial operations, thereby facilitating the digital transformation of rural industries. Guangdong concentrated on establishing a specialized information service framework that is both supported by the government and steered by market dynamics, thus ensuring the sustainability of rural informatization. To become an exemplary province in rural informatization, Hunan ventured into the integrated development of rural industries. Its scheme could be characterized by a unified approach augmented by one body and two wings, the integration of three networks, the amalgamation of resources, the extension of

Six-sector Industrialization of Agriculture: TTF's Innovation and Entrepreneurship in the New Era

services, and the convergence of industries.

The TTF has embraced digital platforms to forge innovative operational frameworks, notably, the "government + cooperatives + enterprises + farmers" model, aimed at exploring rural applications of the fourth sector. Despite these efforts, leveraging digital platforms for rural industrial growth have brought to light several challenges for the TTF. These challenges span from strategic conceptual gaps to shortages of digital technology and marketing talent to product and service standardization issues. How the TTF can better utilize digital technologies to empower rural fourth-sector development has become a significant topic in the digital era. The key lies in nurturing a digital mindset, creating personalized industries and customized services, offering platform-based solutions, fostering Internet+ industries, and cultivating a culture of sharing, collaboration, and systematic management.

Q2: How to Cultivate a Digital Mindset among the TTF?

The fourth sector is propelled by digital technologies, anchored in platform-based business models, directed by the need for personalized and customized products, and centered around data concerning the entire supply chain. This new sector entails a deep integration and reorganization of the primary, secondary, and tertiary sectors, and serves as a stepping stone to the sixth sector. Unlike conventional sectors, the fourth sector, epitomized by "Internet +" industries, harnesses data as a new factor of

production. Just as conventional production factors like land undergo processing to yield value, data requires processing to become actionable knowledge. So the fourth sector leverages data for information and knowledge operations within a platform economy framework. To be more precise, this sector does not just gather information; it also systematically applies such information to develop insights and solutions. The emergence of technologies such as big data, cloud computing, edge computing, and AI marks the constant evolution of the fourth sector. These technologies facilitate the conversion of raw data into valuable insights, embodying the fourth sector's operational approach. In the digital era, innovative business models like live commerce, e-commerce platforms, content e-commerce, and short-form video entertainment are gaining momentum in rural areas. Against such a backdrop, the TTF should avoid sticking to old practices and instead adopt the platform mindset, user experience mindset, and industrial integration mindset.

Platform mindset. Platforms are not a by-product of the digital era; their origins stretch far back in history. From ancient marketplaces to modern shopping centers, each of these things serves as a platform in its own right. Platforms function as intermediaries or brokers within "Internet +" industries, primarily aiming to bridge supply with demand in either bilateral or multilateral markets, thereby generating value for all parties involved through the exchange of goods, services, or social

Six-sector Industrialization of Agriculture: TTF's Innovation and Entrepreneurship in the New Era

capital[①]. The symbiotic relationship between the supply and demand sides on these platforms lead to a network effect. Particularly, digital platforms are instrumental in enhancing rural technology access by aggregating resources, fostering effective resource allocation, and facilitating open sharing. These platforms streamline the processes involved in the agricultural sector—from production and transportation to processing and services—and help improve the crop varieties, product quality, brand image, and standardization level. For example, e-commerce platforms break down the constraints of space and time, allowing global users to trade agricultural products with just a click on their digital devices. Specifically, "Internet + agriculture" information service platforms offer dynamic data for farming, production, processing, and sales, effectively reducing the risks tied to information asymmetry. Agri-product electronic trading platforms provide online trading and market analysis services, thus mitigating the risks of price fluctuations. And agri-product quality standards development platforms are committed to regulating the entire industry chain from breeding, production, and processing to distribution.

User experience mindset. This mindset prioritizes the consideration of users' interactions, emotions, and attitudes towards products and services. It highlights the need to comprehend users' values, perceptions, and interests via human-computer interaction, thereby fostering a consumer experience that stands out from

---

① 〔美〕杰奥夫雷·G. 帕克、马歇尔·W. 范·埃尔斯泰恩、桑基特·保罗·邱达利：《平台革命：改变世界的商业模式》，志鹏译，机械工业出版社，2017，第 43~48 页。

the conventional outcomes of industrial production. From the perspective of consumer experience, the "Internet + agriculture" model signifies a shift towards a new agricultural economy. Placing consumers and value-added services at the center, this model caters to the evolving preferences of users through both tangible and intangible offerings. As material and cultural standards rise, people are seeking products and services that not only meet basic needs but also enhance the quality of life. The consumption of agricultural goods has morphed into an experience where every step, from ordering to usage, is part of the value offered. User expectations are evolving towards more personalized, customized, and digitally integrated products and services. For example, a food company in Weifang, Shandong has rejuvenated the hawthorn industry, previously overlooked by farmers due to its low added value. Embracing contemporary consumer philosophies, the company has intensified R&D in organic, additive-free products, uncovering the health and medicinal virtue of hawthorn and further enhancing its added value. The healthy hawthorn industry park built by the company integrates deep processing with the concept of green, natural, organic, and healthy food. It drives the standardized and integrated development of the hawthorn industry while contributing to rural tourism.

Industrial integration mindset. Industrial integration is driven by scientific, technological, and institutional innovation. At its heart, this integration involves cross-border integration to foster systematic decision-making, enhance secondary business

operations, and ultimately create added value. Bolstered by digital technologies and platforms, the "Internet + agriculture" model uses data as a key factor of production to extend the agricultural chain across production, distribution, sales, information services, and leisure activities, aiming for integrated development of rural industries and value augmentation. Take the cultivation of traditional Chinese medicinal materials as an example. Building on the evolution from cultivation (the primary sector) to processing (the secondary sector) to the deep processing of functional food products, new technologies such as the Internet and e-commerce platforms can help foster "Internet + agriculture" industries, thereby creating added value. For example, during the cultivation of traditional Chinese medicinal materials, adopting an "Internet+ smart agriculture" approach allows rural households to manage environmental factors such as water, nutrients, and climate through mobile apps, promoting standardization, digitization, and quality improvements at the source. In the processing phase, a traceability system based on QR codes can improve brand recognition by enhancing control over products at the factory gate and prior to their market entry. During the sales phase, digital platforms facilitate connections between health management entities and consumers. By enhancing the supply of medicinal products in line with consumer needs, these platforms seamlessly integrate with health and medical industries, extending the industry chain and bringing extra benefits.

Q3: How to Find Platforms of the Fourth Sector, and Their Services?

People might ask, "Should we develop four-sector agricultural platforms first, or leverage existing fourth-sector platforms for agricultural services?" Surely, there is no need to go out of the way to build platforms and see what we can do about them. By adopting a digital mindset, the TTF can focus on identifying existing fourth-sector platforms and using them for agricultural entrepreneurship.

First, establish an agricultural data chain. The TTF should leverage fourth-sector platforms to gradually establish an agricultural data chain. In line with consumer needs, the TTF may begin with amassing extensive data from various sources—including large plantations, cooperatives, processing companies, and commercial businesses—alongside R&D, design, production, processing, and trade statistics. The integration of these data resources helps to balance supply with demand, facilitating reasonable planning for the production, processing, distribution, and consumption of agri-products. This, in turn, boosts the economic gains for all stakeholders, streamlines the agricultural chain, and further elevates the value of farm produce. Only by integrating supply chain data with information from consumers and other stakeholders, and creating a data chain that encompasses the supply chain, value chain, and stakeholder chain, can we precisely align market demand with every aspect of the industrial chain and enhance the network effect and production efficiency. Consequently,

the TTF should cultivate the ability and mindset required for establishing an agricultural data chain, and operating and managing such data based on existing platforms.

Second, promote the integration of industries and platforms. Leveraging fourth-sector platforms, producers can more easily and cost-effectively tailor their offerings to customer needs using digital and intelligent technologies. This approach enables deep integration and collaboration across the supply chain, surpassing the traditional amalgamation of the primary, secondary, and tertiary sectors. By establishing a data chain encompassing multiple industries, we can create standardized interfaces and provide access to credit, insurance, and customer engagement experiences. This facilitates the formation of shared digital platforms with economies of scale and the network effect. The creation of such a data chain promotes the free flow and reorganization of information and resources among the primary, secondary, and tertiary sectors, indicating a move towards the convergence of industries and platforms. This not only fosters the integrated development of these sectors but also aligns resource supply with demand through these platforms, thus opening up new opportunities for increasing the value of agriculture. Hence, the integrated development of rural industries necessitates investments not only in physical infrastructure like industrial parks and leading enterprises but also in the data chain, platforms, and smart technologies. The essence of this investment in "software" is to merge industries with platforms.

Last but not least, enhance the experience of users. User

experience refers to the emotions and attitudes generated during the process of using a product or service. The ecology within the platform model constitutes an open ecosystem that encompasses not only the involvement and experience of users in the development of products and services but also the sharing of relevant customer information, opinion participation on the platform, as well as the interconnection resulting from the opening of platform access subjects and the data sharing among upstream and downstream enterprises. For instance, Haier, being one of the enterprises with the largest number of "lighthouse factories" among Chinese enterprises, has successfully cultivated four "lighthouse factories" through its independently innovative industrial Internet platform-COSMO, emerging as the first industrial Internet platform worldwide to introduce users to engage in the entire process experience. Relying on the platform, users can participate in all aspects of Haier's production and manufacturing, and Haier achieves seamless, transparent and visual user interaction in all production aspects. Through big data analysis of all equipment, Haier precisely responds to user demands and realizes the interconnection among users and factories, users and network devices, and users and the entire process. Why have agricultural products like garlic shoots, ginger, rice, and broad-bean paste featured by Li Ziqi on her short video platform gone viral? The answer lies not just in the products themselves but in the stories they carry. These stories deeply resonate with viewers, showcasing the value that content services can add.

Q4: How Can Digital Platforms Contribute to Sales?

Promote agricultural services through fourth-sector platforms. The TTF should focus on forging partnerships with digital platforms to enhance service reach. First, utilize digital platforms to amass production factors and competitive resources within a specified region, and connect governments, research institutes, and leading enterprises to a broad base of farmers and consumers. This is conducive to transparent virtual communication and interaction among all parties on the platforms. Furthermore, it facilitates systematic analysis using extensive data gathered on the platforms along with computing power and algorithms, so as to grasp the supply-demand dynamics and the competitive industrial landscape, thereby helping innovative businesses with precision marketing. Second, rely on digital technologies to dissect the personalized needs of consumers, and help innovative businesses customize their marketing strategies. Third, leverage the platforms' ability to gather and distribute resources. Enhance the promotion of agricultural products and services through a blend of online and offline channels, including trade shows, mall sales, e-commerce marketing, direct ordering from production bases, tourism-driven promotions, and publicity campaigns. Enable online ordering with the option of in-store collection, and capitalize on the trends of group buying, live commerce, and flash sales. These approaches ensure consumers can easily access high-quality agricultural goods from the comfort of their homes. Last but not least, maximize the platforms' network

effect and economies of scale. Employ digital publicity and marketing tools to broaden the customer base and amplify brand influence.

Develop the innovative model of digital contract farming. Digital platforms act as intermediaries by aligning the needs of the demand side—including a vast array of product and service consumers and logistics entities—with those of the supply side, which comprises farmers, cooperatives, agricultural production and processing firms, and innovative rural businesses. These platforms play a pivotal role in ensuring the agricultural products' quality and represent farmers or innovative businesses during negotiations with buyers, effectively addressing quality issues and reducing risks tied to small-scale farming. Furthermore, digital platforms and tools enable precise market analysis and positioning, which in turn lead to "production on demand" practices. Similarly, digital and intelligent technologies turn "distribution on demand" into reality. The TTF should steer the growth of the primary, secondary, and tertiary sectors toward branding, expansion, standardization, and integration, all propelled by consumer demands. In such a context, the innovative model of digital contract farming is able to transform rural resources, regional traits, and local specialties into industries. Traditionally, local specialties were seen as part of a "long tail market" that was challenging to expand. Now, with the support of digital platforms, the supply and demand sides can be matched efficiently and economically, enabling the industrialization of this previously untapped market.

Leverage platforms to establish distinctive brands. In the development of rural industries, the TTF should focus on selecting high-quality varieties to enhance product quality and build unique brands. These brands should highlight their superior attributes, product excellence, and compelling stories. For the creation of specialty products, tourism products, and cultural products, local strengths—such as featured industries, natural resources, historical and cultural heritage, and ethnic diversity—can serve as a catalyst for industrial chain expansion. In the meantime, digital platforms provide green channels for brand building. The "farmers + e-commerce enterprises + platforms" model enables the utilization of established market channels and operational mechanisms to forge direct links between agricultural producers and consumers, minimizing intermediary expenses and increasing farmers' incomes. The "farmers + cooperatives + e-commerce enterprises + industrial bases" model facilitates industrial expansion, standardization, and branding. It enhances agricultural product quality, diversifies sales avenues, and significantly underpins rural industrial growth. Additionally, leveraging e-commerce platforms to establish regional public brands with cultural or ethnic characteristics can optimize the rural industrial framework and further accelerate rural revitalization.

Create fourth-sector platforms with regional characteristics when conditions are ripe. As digital platform services extend into rural areas, the TTF should embrace a digital mindset to gather regional, industrial, cultural, and creative data by developing an

agricultural digitization industry chain. This chain should bridge various stakeholders including urban, and rural communities, governments, businesses, and farmers, facilitating the formation of ecological assets required for fostering fourth-sector platforms. First, the TTF ought to leverage universal platforms for innovation and entrepreneurship, and in the meantime cultivate an ecosystem for the establishment of fourth-sector platforms. Notably, universal platforms could also be eco-partners. If an ecosystem can effectively and economically pool and allocate platform resources for secondary or multiple data operation cycles, it will be able to establish fourth-sector platforms that embody regional traits. In essence, the fourth-sector platforms built by the TTF act as "small platforms" linked with "large platforms", i.e. universal platforms. It is the synergies between small and large platforms that form an ecosystem dedicated to serving San Nong.

Q5: How to Foster Sharing, Cooperation, and Systematic Management?

Increase the benefits of industrial integration. By leveraging digital platforms to integrate supply chain data with information from consumers and other stakeholders and create a data chain that encompasses the supply chain, value chain, and stakeholder chain, we can precisely align market demand with every aspect of the industrial chain and enhance the network effect and production efficiency. Consider the rural healthcare and wellness market. Digital platforms connect rural TCM cultivation companies and

Six-sector Industrialization of Agriculture: TTF's Innovation and Entrepreneurship in the New Era

medicinal and edible plants processing enterprises with industries like healthcare, pharmaceuticals, and elder care. These platforms not only bridge the gap between supply and demand but also amass data from all stakeholders, placing data management at the heart of fostering collaboration, sharing, and systematic operation. Data management paves the way for the establishment of incentive mechanisms, facilitating profit sharing and collaborative utilization. Furthermore, we need to address specific challenges and requirements. Within a manageable scope, we may pilot the sharing of health data with certain levels and types of medical institutions, drug R&D firms, financial agencies, and academics for profit. Through the development and application of data, we will be able to develop new technologies, products, and services, establish malls specializing in eldercare and wellness, introduce novel industry models, steer consumer trends, and create new value, thereby cultivating a healthcare and wellness ecosystem with strong user stickiness.

Foster talent with digital expertise and interdisciplinary knowledge. In the era of big data, rural areas are facing the challenge of "hollowing out" and pressing demand for new kinds of technical professionals, particularly those with digital expertise and interdisciplinary knowledge. There is a severe gap in rural digital acumen, technological proficiency, and operational experience. In response, institutions of higher learning should overhaul the agricultural economics theory system and further integrate big data and IT into agricultural economics courses, aiming to meet the

socioeconomic demands and nurture talent who are both specialized and versatile. The "Internet + agriculture" model requires efforts to boost digital talent through a variety of stakeholders, approaches, platforms, and methodologies. Likewise, a collaborative push from governments, institutions of higher learning, and innovative businesses is needed to establish rural digital talent development platforms, thereby enhancing the data operation skills of those working in the "Internet + agriculture" sector. A case in point is the Wenchuan E-commerce College initiative, which emerged from a partnership between the Yiwu Municipal Bureau of Commerce, Wenchuan County Bureau of Economy, Commerce, and Information Technology, Yiwu Industrial & Commercial College, and Aba Teachers University. By adopting an approach that encompasses lectures, company visits, studio experiences, and entrepreneurship coaching, this initiative has significantly contributed to the nurturing of e-commerce professionals.

Establish a mechanism for win-win cooperation and sharing. Current models of rural production and organization are largely based on collaboration between leading enterprises, professional cooperatives, family farms, and innovative businesses. Eyeing economies of scale, these models seek to form agricultural alliances with mutual interests as a unifying force. These alliances promote a collaborative work structure across the industrial chain, refine mechanisms based on shared benefits, and support value chain enhancement, thereby deepening integrated industrial development. Furthermore, it is essential to further explore the "Internet +

agriculture" concept to amplify the dual effects of industrial integration and highlight the potential for value generation through the secondary use of data. The "farmers + e-commerce enterprises+ platforms" model enables the utilization of established market channels and operational mechanisms to forge direct links between agricultural producers and consumers, minimizing intermediary expenses and increasing farmers' incomes. The "farmers + cooperatives + e-commerce enterprises + industrial bases" model facilitates industrial scale development, standardization, and branding. It enhances agricultural product quality, diversifies sales avenues, and significantly underpins rural industrial growth. Additionally, leveraging e-commerce platforms and industrial bases to establish brands with cultural or ethnic characteristics can optimize the rural industrial framework and bolster local businesses.

Develop new rural industry models based on systematic management. Conduct market-oriented industry planning, actively cultivate featured agricultural industries with competitive resources and significant market potential, and ensure the provision of distinctive, high-quality farm produce to match consumer needs. Utilize Internet technologies and platforms to maximize the market's role in resource distribution, accelerate online-offline integration to enhance the linkage between the consumers and producers of agricultural products, increase the employment opportunities and incomes of farmers, and lessen the disparity between urban and rural areas. Establish the "Internet + agriculture" frameworks for production and industrial operations. Leverage

e-commerce platforms as well as modern technologies and applications like big data, cloud computing, AI, and blockchain to deepen the integrated development of digital technologies and the agricultural sector. Provide fresh impetus for new industry models such as digital agriculture and e-commerce agriculture, hasten the digital transformation and development of rural industries, and step up efforts to retool the agricultural technology system, so as to boost agricultural productivity, smarten up agricultural management, and improve the quality and effectiveness of rural industrial development. Also, put shared agriculture and digital contract farming on a fast track and further the construction of a modern agricultural industry framework to harmoniously blend the digital economy with rural industries.

Chapter VI   The Fifth Sector as a New Source of Momentum for Innovation and Entrepreneurship of the Technical Task Force (TTF)

Q1: What is the Fifth Sector?

The fifth sector is centered on the new mainstream of consumption, rooted in scientific knowledge and cultural insights, and propelled forward by the power of data. It operates on user experience, with creative storytelling as a key method of engagement. Within this innovative realm, two critical elements have given shape to a new business paradigm. (1) Data-driven scientific intelligence. In a departure from the technologization of science, the fifth sector advances along the path of data-driven scientific intelligence. Under the triple helix model of innovation, scientific knowledge can be directly applied to industries via data. This is particularly relevant for new scientific paradigms represented by AGI. AGI combines explicit knowledge (related to technology), tacit knowledge (understanding market opportunities), and implicit knowledge (requiring AI and machine interpretation) to fuel a virtuous cycle of innovation across science, AI, and market applications. It

identifies consumer needs through efficient collection, analysis, and application of data. Furthermore, through self-learning and adaptation, AGI is able to create new knowledge, products, and services. (2) Cultural and creative output. The fifth sector also taps into the inherently qualitative nature of culture to weave engaging narratives that emotionally connect with consumers. It aims to enrich and manage user experiences based on novel business paradigms formed under the triple helix model of innovation.

Traditional cultural and creative industries are centered around arts, music, films, and literature. Following industrialization models, these industries typically feature artists, creators, and cultural institutions, and derive economic benefits through the creation and distribution of cultural products, including traditional handicrafts, drama performances, fine arts, music, publications, and audio-visual content.

In the post-materialistic era, people striving for a higher quality of life will increasingly focus on emotional fulfillment. This will lead to a transformation in the way value chains are designed, with a greater emphasis placed on non-material aspirations. Cultural and creative output plays a pivotal role in addressing emotional and cultural requirements. It stands as a key source of added value in this new era. An example of this is the incorporation of filial piety, a core aspect of traditional Chinese culture, into value chains. The digital age necessitates novel strategies and frameworks for the fulfillment of emotional and cultural needs. For a culture-rich nation

like China, the exploration of fresh industry models that meet the non-material needs of contemporary society holds both theoretical and practical significance.

The fifth sector diverges from traditional cultural and creative industries by tapping into unique value-creation mechanisms. In the industrial era, cultural and creative industries extracted added value by embedding cultural factors into tangible offerings. This model dictated that commercial value was contingent upon creativity materializing in physical products or quantifiable services. Books, CDs, and handicrafts are classic examples where the value is intrinsically linked to tangible forms. The fifth sector shifts its focus towards the individual, centering its commercial essence on the cultivation of user experience. This sector transcends the confines of physical products and traditional services, embracing intangible avenues like online platforms, virtual experiences, and community interactions. It employs scientific intelligence as well as cultural and creative expressions to craft personalized experiences that cater to users' emotional demands. For example, Li Ziqi and Dong Yuhui have intertwined their eco-products with cultural and creative narratives that emotionally engage and drive market appeal. Innovative methods of value creation enable the fifth sector to navigate the dynamic market landscape with agility, tap into the deeper emotional and value appeal of consumers, and thereby generate added value.

User experience (UX) is characterized by both horizontal and vertical interconnections. Many elements of user experience can

be integrated into an organic whole. For instance, parent-child educational experiences merge education, leisure travel, and unique craftsmanship smoothly. In the orchestration of user experience, traditional industry boundaries are removed. As to the vertical (or temporal) interconnections of user experience, let's take a look at healthcare. Healthcare spans a continuum of user experiences over time, such as health management, diagnosis and treatment, and post-operative care. These experiences require the integration of relevant industries at different stages. Moving beyond the traditional focus on tangible goods as vessels for emotional value, UXblends the roles of consumers and producers through active engagement and the incorporation of community networks. Therefore, cross-industrial business ecosystems stand out as a hallmark of fifth-sector operational models.

The fifth sector introduces a new factor, intelligence, to traditional cultural and creative industries. During the industrial age, the traditional factors are still land, capital, and labor, which reflects the characteristics of a three-sector economy. In contrast, the fifth sector builds upon the fourth sector's reliance on data and introduces the factor of intelligence, including scientific intelligence as well as cultural and creative output. Today's consumers are willing to pay for creative experiences, familial joy, and emotional satisfaction. Consequently, the fifth sector seeks to connect on an emotional level and help consumers realize their dreams. For example, Pop Mart elevates its role beyond merely producing toys by delivering an element of surprise to consumers, thereby

generating additional value. This concept can be compared to the following analogy. I would not contemplate spending RMB 10000 on rice, irrespective of its quantity. However, if the rice vendor provided extraordinary care for my mother, I might be tempted to make a RMB 100000 purchase for her sake. As you can see, the ability to satisfy emotional desires amplifies the value of a product.

The fifth sector leverages data to pioneer new channels of media communication, giving rise to unprecedented industrial forms and business models. Despite the historical value of traditional channels and forms of cultural and artistic expression, they fall short of satisfying modern societal demands and trends. Anchored in digitalization, intelligence, and ecosystemization, the fifth sector prioritizes cross-industrial fusion and innovation, aiming for the integration and transformation of the entire industry chain. For example, it has ushered in novel art forms such as digital painting, digital music, and digital cinema, alongside innovative business models like Internet-based art trading platforms, online music services, and video streaming platforms. These art forms and business models not only harbor higher commercial value but also attract a wider audience and possess greater market potential. Breaking free from conventional thinking, the fifth sector enables the swift actualization of creative concepts at minimal costs via AGI, thus facilitating access to new markets and spheres.

Q2: Why is the Fifth Sector Necessary for Rural Revitalization?

In the industrial era, the evolution of rural regions was primarily propelled by agriculture and handicrafts, with a marked absence of cultural and creative factors. Several obstacles hampered rural development as outlined below. (1) Structural limitations. The backbone of the rural economy was agriculture and traditional crafts. These industries focused on enhancing production efficiency and scaling up rather than fostering cultural innovation and customization. (2) Data deficiency. Rural areas often faced challenges in catering to the needs of different groups due to a scarcity of data. This led to a superficial understanding of target demographics and consumption patterns, complicating efforts to accurately communicate the characteristics and value of products or services. (3) Constrained communication channels. The spread of information in rural areas was largely dependent on conventional media and word-of-mouth. This limited the reach and influence of cultural and creative works. Even the outstanding ones found it hard to gain extensive visibility and appreciation. (4) Lack of infrastructure and business ecosystems. Rural areas were devoid of important infrastructure like cultural exchange platforms and creative industry parks, which impeded the incubation and development of cultural and creative industries. Moreover, the climate for investing in these industries was notably weak, with a dearth of necessary talent, funding, and technology. These factors

collectively stymied the advancement and commercial success of rural cultural and creative industries.

In 2018, the CPC Central Committee and the State Council issued the Rural Revitalization Strategy (2018-2022), which sets out the general requirement of building rural areas with thriving businesses, pleasant living environments, social etiquette and civility, effective governance, and prosperity. One of China's primary tasks at this stage is to consolidate and expand the achievements of poverty alleviation and effectively integrate it with rural revitalization, thereby accelerating the modernization of agriculture and rural areas. While both poverty alleviation and rural revitalization aim to improve the conditions of San Nong, the former focuses on meeting basic needs such as food and clothing, and the latter is concerned with wealth creation. Specifically, rural revitalization efforts seek to improve the quality and efficiency of agricultural production, make rural areas more suitable for work and living, and help farmers get rich. Given the advancement of technologies and the widespread adoption of the Internet, rural residents now desire a high-quality cultural life and access to a variety of entertainment options, just as their urban counterparts do.

As a time-honored civilization, China's rural areas possess abundant cultural resources. Empowering rural revitalization with culture means holistically incorporating the cultural industry into the national strategy. This approach requires establishing a new development paradigm that synergizes industry, talent, markets,

and cultural assets, devising rural policies in line with local characteristics, encouraging cultural institutions and creators to actively participate in the building of rural culture, and showcasing the new allure of rural areas. It is imperative to expand the cultural industry, thoroughly explore the essence of traditional Chinese culture, and further implement the rural revitalization strategy based on innovative business models.

Under business models fueled by digital innovation, entrepreneurship within the fifth sector stands out as a critical force in defining the mainstream trends of the future. The rapid development of IT and its intelligent applications breathe new life into rural areas, facilitating the spread of information, sharing of resources, and transformation of industries. On the other hand, business ecosystems that revolve around cultural and creative factors foster the seamless blending of various industries, which in turn invigorates the rural economy.

The TTF is expected to constantly broaden its horizons and stay abreast of the times. In the realm of rural revitalization, TTF who opt not to explore entrepreneurial opportunities within the fifth sector risk overlooking the significant potential value it holds. While traditional entrepreneurial ventures can still find success, their impact might be constrained if they do not leverage the opportunities for value creation presented by the new mainstream.

Q3: How to Uncover the Cultural and Creative Value of the Fifth Sector?

To answer this question, we must first figure out what user experience is. User experience encompasses how a product or service fulfills individuals' emotional and aspirational desires, delivering feelings of joy, satisfaction, and connection during its use. This emotional connection encourages a stronger identification with the product or service, boosting loyalty and the likelihood of users recommending it to others. Creating a compelling user experience requires users' active engagement. Their involvement and interaction at each phase of product or service usage help customize and enrich their experience. A case in point is LEGO Ideas, a platform that empowers enthusiasts to create and submit their LEGO model concepts. Other users can vote on these submissions, and with enough support, LEGO may opt to manufacture them as official sets. This approach facilitates comprehensive user involvement, enabling them to participate in the design and production of LEGO products.

Outstanding cultural and creative products can meet users' emotional needs not only in the real world but also in virtual environments. For example, in the VR game "The Sims", players have the opportunity to design and manage the lives of their virtual personas, achieving aspirations that might be challenging to attain in the real world. As they nurture their families, advance in their professions, and chase their ambitions, players are immersed in a

distinctive and enticing experience.

In the fifth sector, user experience is also closely linked to social interaction. Products or services can enhance users' sense of participation and belonging by allowing them to share their feelings via social platforms or interactive experiences. For example, on apps like WeChat, which everyone uses, along with Weibo, Zhihu, Xiaohongshu, Instagram, and Facebook, users can communicate with their friends, family, and other users by posting photos or videos.

Case Study: Little Miss Matched's Disruptive Creativity

Little Miss Matched is a US retail chain specializing in socks. Unlike traditional pairs, each set from Little Miss Matched boasts distinct designs, which turn these socks into collectibles that resonate particularly with girls who have a keen eye for aesthetics. The brand's strategy is as follows: capture its audience's attention with disruptive creativity, delivering delightful surprises to foster an emotional connection with its consumers. Within just two years, Little Miss Matched has sold over 600000 pairs. It now owns 600 specialty stores, with its asset value reaching USD 100 million.

The rise of Little Miss Matched serves as a compelling lesson for traditional industries: innovation breakthrough points and business opportunities can sometimes be found in industries perceived as static. The brand exemplifies a full cycle of market disruption. (1) Formulate a disruptive hypothesis. The conventional practices

of selling socks in pairs represent a "natural law" that Little Miss Matched boldly challenges. (2) Spot a disruptive opportunity. Focusing on girls aged 8-12, who are navigating the transition from childhood to adolescence, Little Miss Matched capitalizes on their playfulness, despite their budding maturity and self-perception as young adults. (3) Implement a disruptive innovation. By offering socks in odd numbers, Little Miss Matched sets itself apart from traditional brands. The brand name itself is layered with meaning, suggesting girls' expertise in creating matches, their penchant for deliberate mismatching in fashion, and a universal sentiment of feeling "out of sync" at times.

(I) How to commercialize and manage user experience

In recent years, utilizing specialty produce for cultural branding has emerged as a prevalent business approach. For instance, synergizing its grape culture with rural tourism, Ningxia has launched grape-picking and wine culture festivals where visitors are encouraged to immerse themselves in the rural lifestyle. Another popular business approach is "culture + tourism", which accentuates the unique local traits through immersive experiences. This approach is vividly illustrated in destinations such as Kuanzhai Alley, where visitors can delve into the authentic old Chengdu lifestyle; Nanjing Fuzimiao, with its scenic Qinhuai River; the Great Tang All Day Mall in Xi'an, which showcases the grandeur of the Tang Dynasty; and Hubin Road in Hangzhou, known for the timeless beauty of

West Lake. Furthermore, governments and NGOs are striving to foster long-term mechanisms for passing down intangible cultural heritage. They have compiled lists of intangible cultural heritage, founded heritage associations, and set up rural cultural preservation organizations to ensure the ongoing vitality of cultural heritage. These efforts are complemented by experiential tourism projects such as experiencing the Naxi ethnic culture of Lijiang and brocade weaving at Qingcheng Mountain.

In contrast to conventional models, digitalization and business ecosystems play a pivotal role in the commercialization of user experience within the fifth sector. Digitalization extends beyond merely supplying technological platforms and tools; it seamlessly integrates scientific intelligence as well as cultural and creative output into market applications, ensuring that user experiences are more personalized and disseminated within a broader area. Business ecosystems create a structured commercial landscape that encompasses supply chains, partners, and resources, thereby providing ongoing support for enhancing user experience and extending the value chain.

With the widespread adoption of digital technologies, user experience extends not just to various offline scenarios but also to mature online business models. Take Douyin as an example. This social media platform has successfully commercialized user experience, offering a diverse range of content to meet users' emotional needs while providing commercial opportunities for advertisers and creators. Douyin fosters an "interest-driven"

e-commerce ecosystem, leveraging a variety of engaging content and algorithmic recommendations to encourage users to explore cost-effective, high-quality products. This approach not only piques consumer curiosity but also spurs purchasing motivation. For the short video industry, the richness of content holds the key to retaining users in the long run. In view of this, platform enterprises are sparing no effort to explore user value.

In the digital era, sales on We Media have become a new pathway for agricultural enterprises to reach the market. We Media platforms, encompassing social networks, blogs, and video and live-streaming services, offer traditional agricultural businesses a direct channel to interact with consumers and market their products. The Yanchi Tan Sheep from Ningxia, a famed traditional livestock specialty in Northwest China, encountered obstacles in conventional sales avenues such as wholesale markets, supermarkets, and retail outlets. These avenues often involve numerous intermediaries, leading to high costs and a disconnect from consumers. To address these challenges, Qiang Fenlin, a sci-tech expert working in Yanchi County, launched an e-commerce platform aimed at promoting Tan Sheep. This platform leverages supply and marketing cooperatives and the Internet to reach a national audience, creating a "breeding-processing-sales" model and directing villagers towards technologies. As an innovative industry model, "live commerce + cooperatives" not only opens up new sales channels for agricultural products but also generates financial gains for farmers.

To manage user engagement, We Media needs to forge an

emotional bond with its audience while respecting social culture. Without this emotional bond, even substantial traffic could instantly disintegrate. Dong Yuhui, who has won the hearts of many through his unique blend of romanticism and talents. With his soothing voice, Dong has the power to deeply move people, bringing them to tears over simple things like a corn cob. What sets Dong apart is his storytelling prowess, which he uses to imbue products with emotional depth and cultural significance, thereby enriching the user experience with meaningful connections. This contrast illustrates the pivotal role of cultural and emotional intelligence in digital engagement. In the fifth sector, any interaction that comes across as dismissive or inappropriate not only damages the user experience but also undermines the foundational cultural and emotional ties.

When it comes to business ecosystems, Disney stands out as a prime example. Disney produces a wide array of audio-visual content, including movies, TV series, and stage plays. Its operations reflect a mix of globalization and localization, demonstrating a commitment to innovation that aligns with contemporary trends. The Disneyland Parks, inspired by Disney's animated features and movies, offer a variety of tourism-related services and facilities and constantly expand their business ventures. Beyond these amusement parks, Disney provides dining options, souvenir shopping, themed resort stays, and internal transportation, aiming to deliver an ideal experience for its visitors.

In terms of profitability, Disney adopts a multi-tiered revenue

model. Initially, revenue is generated through the box office success of its films and blockbuster animations. Following this, the company capitalizes on the earnings from film and video sales and rentals. The third phase involves leveraging new movie characters or animated figures to draw visitors to its theme parks, offering them an ideal, fairy-tale-like experience. The fourth revenue stream emerges from merchandising and brand licensing. Additionally, Disney constantly acquires prominent media assets, harnessing the power of TV to amplify the appeal and visibility of its merchandise. This approach ensures the seamless operation of Disney's brand value chain.

Case Study: Selecting Wedding Items on Zola

A wedding gift shopping website from the US, Zola sets itself apart with a "wedding registry" feature. This feature replicates the offline wedding preparation experience online, providing a unique platform where users can register, upload photos, and create lists of desired wedding gifts ranging from kitchenware and food to furniture. It also offers a communal space for friends and family to view these lists and contribute to a wedding preparation fund. Zola has successfully carved out a significant presence in the vertical e-commerce market for wedding items. Through the integration of online social experiences, Zola manages to enhance user engagement, thereby distinguishing itself from traditional competitors and gaining favor in the capital market.

Zola's standout feature for its intended audience lies in its ability to help them craft a more captivating and heartfelt wedding narrative. This enhanced storytelling serves to deeply resonate with the guests and friends at the wedding celebration. Zola allows users to build customized sites, where they can post photos with text or curate a list of coveted presents. Wedding guests may contribute towards these gifts, which may range from everyday items to a house, on those sites. Zola's profit model includes a 40% commission on physical goods sold through the platform, an approx. 20% fee for experiential services, and a 2.7% processing charge on monetary gifts.

Q4: How Can Digitalization Empower Rural Cultural and Creative Industries?

(I) What new changes have digitalization brought to rural cultural and creative industries?

The robust development of digital technologies has profoundly invigorated and transformed rural cultural and creative industries. Furthermore, the digitization wave has opened up unparalleled opportunities and tapped into the infinite potential of rural revitalization. The appealing living environments and deep-rooted history and culture of rural areas serve as a fertile ground for cultural and creative expressions. Through digital means, rural folk customs, handicrafts, and artistic performances can be accurately

Six-sector Industrialization of Agriculture: TTF's Innovation and Entrepreneurship in the New Era

recorded and broadly shared. Interactive technologies such as VR and AR offer people the opportunity to deeply immerse themselves in the rural environment, thus fostering a profound interest in and appreciation for local culture. Take "Digital Qiannan" for example. By digitally amassing and amalgamating local cultural heritage, this program has successfully set up an online platform for cultural heritage preservation. The platform encompasses the digital library, digital exhibition hall, digital cultural products, and relevant data. By showcasing culture in a digital format, the program increases the fame and impact of local customs, stimulates the growth of the local cultural tourism industry, and injects fresh energy into the local economy.

Most importantly, digitization drives the integration of rural cultural and creative industries with others, transcending the conventional industry barriers. Through digital technologies, rural cultural and creative industries realize deep collaborations with tourism, agriculture, catering, and other related industries. For example, digitally empowered rural events that feature a blend of agricultural, cultural, and creative products hold greater appeal to tourists and consumers alike. Cross-industrial collaborations not only promote multifaceted growth of the rural economy but also carve new avenues and provide fresh opportunities for the sustainable development of rural areas.

(II) How to spread the fascinating stories of rural areas through digital means?

Rural communities should harness cultural resources, digital technologies, and new advertising platforms to tell fascinating

stories. Specifically, advertising has transitioned from a one-way communication model dependent on newspapers and TV to a more interactive and community-focused model propelled by the Internet and mobile technologies.

Li Ziqi has successfully established herself as a leading figure in the inheritance and transmission of traditional Chinese rural culture. As a former top Internet celebrity in the culinary world, she has become Chengdu's ambassador for intangible cultural heritage promotion. Li Ziqi's videos mainly illustrate the art of traditional culinary practices alongside her skilled handiwork in crafting rouge, dyeing fabrics, and creating clothing. She also delves into the craftsmanship behind the Four Treasures of the Study. China's pastoral landscapes feature prominently in her videos, which frequently portray her engaged in agricultural activities or within rustic settings, wearing Hanfu. As noted by *China Newsweek*, Li Ziqi is a dream-maker in real life. Against the backdrop of rural brooks and the cyclic beauty of the seasons, her work vividly brings to life the traditional and genuine lifestyle of the Chinese populace, offering a touchstone of spiritual kinship for modern city-dwellers while fostering cultural comprehension among a global audience. Through her portrayal, both daily meals and the rhythm of changing seasons are imbued with deeper aesthetic value, illustrating the dynamic energy brought by physical labor.

Short video platforms have been amplifying their support for creations in rural settings. The prominence of "rural Internet celebrities" such as Li Ziqi in mainstream media highlights short

videos as powerful channels for rural individuals to showcase their lifestyles, seek acknowledgment of their social identities, and share their local cultures. These channels meet the inherent need for self-expression among rural residents. For those who are less skilled in written communication, short videos have emerged as a crucial means of entertainment and self-expression in their everyday lives. Meanwhile, urban audiences engage with the multiple dimensions of rural culture by commenting on or sharing short videos or interacting with the creators, thus fulfilling their curiosity and rebuilding collective memories of rural living.

In addition to top anchors like Li Ziqi, a group of TTF is capitalizing on the digital economy boom. Employing digital tools and short video platforms, they are engaged in innovation and entrepreneurship in rural areas, driving the advancement of smart farming. YChina, the first Internet information TTF engaged by Wuyishan City in Fujian Province, is a prime example. Comprising young video creators from both China and abroad, this team immersed themselves in the local mechanized tea harvesting and production process. They also crafted a video to promote the "Wu Yi Shan Shui" tea brand globally. The video quickly amassed a large audience online, igniting a movement towards experiencing Wuyishan's tea firsthand.

(III) How to keep the momentum after a surge in traffic?

Many online creations swiftly capture considerable attention but tend to fade into obscurity over time. Transforming fleeting traffic into enduring loyalty necessitates profound cooperation based on

the fifth sector. The distinct charm of cultural and creative output has gradually become a new economic driver. Fueled by innovation and anchored in cultural heritage, the fusion of technology and arts generates content and brand identities that are more captivating, providing unparalleled experiences to audiences.

Consumption represents both a lifestyle and a productive force. The urban identity of Chengdu has extended beyond its iconic association with the giant panda to include connections to the Three Kingdoms, Jinsha site, local cuisine, and Sichuan opera. During the 2023 National Day holiday, Chengdu highlighted the emerging concept of "City Walk", focusing on leisure, slow-paced, and immersive experiences. This approach resonates with modern consumers who value immersion, social engagement, and lifestyle aesthetics. Additionally, Chengdu has capitalized on its role as a tourism gateway to Sichuan by expanding themed travel routes. This includes cultural tourism projects like night tours along the Jinjiang River and featured bus journeys, with the aim of broadening the city's cultural appeal. Chengdu's strategy involves constantly shifting from traditional to new industry models and scenarios. The emphasis on social, immersive, and interactive experiences in consumption settings is emerging as a new mainstream trend.

Zibo barbecue serves as an exemplary case of how cultural appeal can transform fleeting traffic into enduring loyalty. In promotional narratives, Zibo is often celebrated as a "hub of heavy industry" and a "city with a deep historical and cultural

lineage". Such portrayals effectively accentuate the city's unique attributes and advantages. The widespread popularity of Zibo barbecue is illustrated through viral content on platforms like Douyin and Weibo, predominantly generated by consumers who are enthused about the affordable delectability of Zibo barbecue and the hospitality of residents. This bears out the significance of experiential sharing in modern communication channels, such as new media and community networks. Additionally, Zibo embraces a digital economy model that leverages online exposure to boost offline engagement, converting the barbecue phenomenon into a new opportunity for the city's progress. Local culture and tourism officials assume roles as "Zibo Culture and Tourism Ambassadors", educating live-stream viewers (e.g. high-speed train passengers) about Zibo barbecue. This approach not only rejuvenates the city's image but also constantly amplifies Zibo's appeal. Furthermore, Zibo's efforts have expanded beyond barbecue promotion to talent attraction, offering incentives like housing and living allowance to young professionals and students. Thus, the allure of Zibo barbecue, drawing innumerable tourists from distant locales, extends beyond its distinctive taste. It is the city's reassuring consumption environment, considerate consumer experience, and exceptionally friendly services that truly resonate. The phenomenon begins with culinary appeal, is underpinned by effective governance, and thrives on a stellar reputation. While the barbecue trend might wane, the accumulated governance insights and enhanced city reputation will serve as valuable resources for Zibo's future development.

Q5: How Can Ecosystemization Reinvigorate Rural Cultural and Creative Industries?

(I) How to build business ecosystems for rural cultural and creative industries?

In recent years, the development of business ecosystems tailored to rural cultural and creative industries has emerged as a pivotal aspect of rural revitalization efforts. With growing interest in rural culture, the innovation and evolution of business models are now central to the growth of cultural and creative projects in rural areas. In this context, a number of standout business ecosystems have come to the fore, breathing new life and economic value into rural cultural and creative industries.

Originally a village sporting event in Rongjiang County, Guizhou Province, a football league initiated by locals has evolved significantly from its grassroots beginnings and rural backdrop. Its swelling popularity has earned it the title "Village Super League", a name inspired by prestigious tournaments, like the Chinese Super League and the English Premier League. A single match within the Village Super League can draw up to 50000 spectators— a figure that starkly contrasts with the average attendance of 24000 for the first round of eight games in the 2023 Chinese Super League. This is particularly striking for a county with merely 380000 people. The Village Super League not only showcases the passion and vitality inherent in rural areas but also demonstrates the unique appeal and unifying force of football, affirming its status as a sport for all.

The significant visibility of the Village Super League can largely be attributed to its focus on digital marketing and its proficient use of online platforms for dissemination. Rongjiang has been particularly effective in leveraging short videos to invite notable football personalities like Fan Zhiyi, Han Qiaosheng, and Huang Jianxiang. Notably, English football star Michael Owen recorded a video extending his best wishes to the league. Additionally, Rongjiang has launched a training program for short video live-streaming, leading to the creation of over 12000 short video accounts and more than 2200 local teams specializing in Internet live commerce. This massive network of new media talent, coupled with tens of thousands of generated videos, has successfully propelled the league's presence on social media platforms, significantly enhancing its popularity and reach.

Another key strategy for drawing crowds to the Village Super League involves capitalizing on local traits to enrich the overall experience. Understanding that viewers primarily look for emotional engagement during the matches, Rongjiang weaves the region's cultural and athletic traditions into the fabric of the league. As the games are set to begin, teams from different villages, adorned in traditional attire and bearing local specialties, parade onto the field with the players, engaging in songs and dances reflective of their heritage. The intermission features a variety of ethnic cultural performances, including the Grand Song of the Dong people and the Lusheng dance of the Miao people. In the awards ceremony, the victors of individual matches receive two pork

knuckles each, while the grand prize for the season's champions is a local yellow cattle. Additionally, the most enthusiastic spectator is awarded a bag of local rice.

Furthermore, in a bid to attract a larger fan base to the matches, Guiyang has introduced direct bus routes to Rongjiang in addition to high-speed railways. This initiative makes weekend excursions to catch the games a practical possibility. Such efforts not only further energize the Village Super League but also catalyze growth in regional industries such as transport, tourism, and catering. Ultimately, it is the residents that benefit from the league.

Sports stands out for its long industry chain and extensive influence. It leverages the widespread appeal of competitive events, together with unique local cultural, ecological, and industrial resources, to forge brands that integrate "competitions, rural tourism, traditional culture, and fitness for all". This strategy fosters a deep integration of sports with agriculture, commerce, and cultural tourism. Furthermore, it draws in leading sporting goods manufacturers and retailers, facilitating the integrated development of competitive events and ethnic customs. It also actively introduces urban cultural and creative talent for rural entrepreneurship, boosting the R&D of themed and trendy products while forging a distinctive sports industry chain.

To sum up, the remarkable rise of the Village Super League would be impossible without new media and supportive local policies. Yet the true driving force behind its transformation

from a village competition to a super league is the people's love for football. For any aspirant region, embracing a people-first strategy, fostering innovation while upholding ethical standards, and developing a well-rounded urban system are key to progress. The triumph of the Village Super League also hinges on substantial governmental backing. In Rongjiang, sporting events transcend mere commercial activities, serving instead their most genuine purpose: to delight and to forge a connection with one's heritage. Here, participation is universal. Everyone is likely to rise as a superstar; everyone has a chance to shine.

(II) What are the new contractual models of business ecosystems?

Equity contracts emerged during the Industrial Age as a solution to improve corporate governance. They were created to bridge the gap between ownership and management, thus addressing the principal-agent problem. By offering equity incentives—granting shares to employees—these contracts aim to align the interests of employees with those of shareholders. Essentially, they act as a mechanism focused on shareholder interests, indirectly benefiting shareholders by encouraging employee involvement.

In the digital era, chain group contracts represent a novel exploration of incentive mechanisms. Here, "chain" refers to the ecosystem chain. Ecosystem chains disrupt traditional hierarchical structures, fostering boundaryless organizations. "Group" refers to the micro cluster along the ecosystem chain. In a boundaryless ecosystem, everyone has a chance to maximize their value through innovation.

The distinctions between chain group contracts and equity contracts can be summarized as follows. (1) Chain group contracts focus on creating value for people across an open ecosystem. By setting overarching goals and allowing open participation, the leader of a chain group enhances user experience and fosters value sharing among all contributors. In contrast, equity contracts typically restrict incentive allocation to a select group of key employees. This makes it difficult to motivate a wider workforce, a challenge that becomes more pronounced in the realm of IoT. (2)Chain group contracts introduce a dynamic incentive model. Unlike equity incentives, which might lead to employee complacency after the acquisition of shares, chain group contracts maintain and increase motivation by setting clear and evolving targets. Individuals who hit the targets will encounter new goals to pursue, while those who fail to do so will be replaced by more appropriate candidates. Equity contracts distribute dividends according to the ownership structure of the contract, so they do not have the dynamic optimization of chain group contracts. (3) Chain group contracts foster a community of shared interests among all stakeholders by necessitating personal investment at every stage, thereby aligning rewards with risks. This is in contrast to equity incentives, where the low risks associated with the acquisition of shares at low costs might not be able to fully align individual contributions with collective goals.

Haier's Fourth Financial Statement

Riding the momentum of its strategic transition in 2021, Haier broke new ground by supplementing the conventional trio of financial statements—balance sheet, income statement, and cash flow statement—with a fourth one, the Win-Win Value Added (WWVA) Statement. The WWVA statement, based on the Rendanheyi management model, incorporates six key elements: user resources, resource providers, the aggregate value of the eco-platform, revenue, cost, and marginal benefit. Designed to dynamically monitor, evaluate, and drive the value creation process with a user-centric approach, the WWVA statement accurately measures value distribution among ecosystem stakeholders, including users, chain groups, resource providers, and Haier itself.

The WWVA statement extends beyond static tangible assets to include intangible user resources, epitomizing a self-evolving ecosystem centered on user experience iteration and lifetime value creation. It also encapsulates the ethos of co-creation and sharing among partners, underscoring the value of a cross-industrial ecosystem where contributions and benefits are aligned.

As Haier deepens its digital transformation, it has created a blockchain-based chain group contract application characterized by "smart contracts, technological empowerment, and comprehensive visualization". This application transitions offline processes for contract signing, implementation of contingency plans, and subsequent sharing of accrued value into an online framework. With

the integration of chain group contracts, the WWVA statement encompasses not just the corporate value determinants like users and resources but also the dimensions of value generation such as platform value, revenue, cost, and marginal benefit. It fosters constant engagement with users, converting their personalized needs into collective and individual goals through chain group contracts.

Q6: Why is "Digitization $\oplus$ Ecosystemization" the Only Way to Develop Future Industries?

Future industries, which typify ecosystem-based industries of the sixth sector, represent new industry models that not only integrate cutting-edge technologies highlighted in China's 14th Five-Year Plan—such as brain-inspired intelligence, quantum information, genetic technology, future network, deep-sea and aerospace exploration, hydrogen energy, and energy storage—but also reshape the way industries operate. Digitally empowered, traditional industries are able to reinvent themselves, adopting novel forms that stand apart from the conventional industrial framework. This transformation is driven by innovative models that thrive within the digital ecosystem. The data sector lays the groundwork for future industries, whereas the fifth sector underpins their profitability and value. Therefore, the innovative development of future industries requires six-sector industrialization, where six-sector industrialization=digitization $\oplus$ ecosystemization.

(I) The Six-sector Theory clarifies the fifth-sector model for metaverse development

"Metaverse" gained significant attention in the capital market after Mark Zuckerberg announced the re-branding of Facebook as Meta.

The advancement of the Internet, AI, and big data in the digital era has undeniably opened up new speculative business opportunities for the metaverse. While the concept of the metaverse might suggest a detachment from the physical realm, the refinement of certain business models within this virtual space is set to create meaningful links with reality.

The current interpretation of the metaverse concept has its limitations. The much-hyped metaverse posits the coexistence of the virtual and physical worlds, implying that the industrial and digital ages are unfolding concurrently. This perception is based on the Three-sector Theory rather than the Six-sector Economy Theory.

The latter argues against dividing the world into two parallel realms. Instead, it envisions a future where the virtual and physical worlds, i.e. the digital and industrial sectors, are increasingly interconnected. The metaverse represents a virtual universe that emerges along with the digital age. However, the Six-sector Economy Theory is still a nascent concept awaiting broader acknowledgment. Without compromising the growth of tangible industries or the industrialization trajectory of our nation, it is advisable to create some virtual world models and promote beneficial interactions between virtual and real economies. Still,

we should stay alert to speculative behaviors, which might cause financial risks or other adverse effects.

The metaverse, shaped by the convergence of contemporary information technologies, has birthed a novel socioeconomic domain where the virtual and physical spaces merge. In this domain, AI serves as both the foundation stone and the content generator; blockchain provides tamper-proof mechanisms for establishing trustworthy consensus; cloud technology offers computational power for metaverse applications; and digital twins grant users 360° immersive and interactive experiences that are richly contextualized within the digital sphere.

The metaverse has realized economic interconnectivity between the digital and physical worlds, thereby establishing a highly digitized and intelligent closed-loop economic system. Data has emerged as the most crucial factor of production within the metaverse. From virtual land and props &equipment to algorithm models and data resources, everything can be transformed into digital assets and circulated in the market to determine their fair value. The integration of blockchain technology in the metaverse, combined with market-driven allocation mechanisms, can maximize the value of data, positioning it as the most important asset within the metaverse.

Epitomizing the industry models of the fifth sector, the metaverse is characterized by its creator-driven nature and the important role of digital content. In this space, users are not only consumers of content but also its creators and distributors, fostering

a development model rooted in community culture. Through the integration of commercial and cultural value, this fifth sector fuels the expansion of the metaverse economy, giving digital culture a big boost. Additionally, the economic fabric of metaverse gaming is woven with a sophisticated system, where assets are commonly represented by Non-Fungible Tokens (NFTs) or digital collectibles. Blockchain technology underpins NFT, providing a framework for authenticating digital assets, thereby enabling their valuation and exchange.

(II) Future agriculture represents the main battleground for the TTF's innovation and entrepreneurship in the new era

Future agriculture marks the six-sector industrialization of agriculture. While traditional farming focused primarily on meeting humanity's basic food and survival requirements, the evolution from agrarian societies to industrial ones highlighted agriculture's role in narrowing the urban-rural gap. In the context of the digital economy, future agriculture may leverage data as a new factor of production. Platforms such as Douyin have profoundly changed how agricultural operations are conducted. The vision for future agriculture extends beyond mere sustenance; it aligns with contemporary lifestyle trends that underscore a deeper quest for emotional and cultural experiences within the agricultural domain. This is evident in the emergence of various integrated models like health agriculture, which combines health and farming; agritourism, where agriculture meets tourism; cultural agriculture, which integrates family education; and carbon farming, which

merges ecological stewardship with agricultural practices. These avant-garde models push past conventional industry limits into an ecological framework that encompasses not only natural but also social (e.g. ESG-based) and business ecosystems.

The evolution of future agriculture necessitates six-sector industrialization. First, recognizing data as a new production element, the agricultural sector can utilize AGI to generate data assets, fostering connections with other sectors. Second, future agriculture should adapt to new mainstream values by prioritizing user experience. This approach involves creating high-value-added industries through VR, AR, as well as dynamic networks that span both physical and virtual realms. Last but not least, blockchain technology and smart contracts enable the agricultural sector to break free from conventional industry limits. They also facilitate the creation of a dual-value loop and the establishment of business ecosystems tailored for the agriculture of tomorrow.

During the poverty alleviation phase, the TTF system was designed to tackle market failures by offering agricultural technologies and services to rural areas, thereby fostering grassroots innovation and entrepreneurship. This phase bore witness to many innovation and entrepreneurship initiatives, such as the Nanping model, Zhejiang's technology-driven poverty alleviation program, Hainan's information-driven approach, Jiangsu's support for "thousands of villages and tens of thousands of households", and Ningxia's entrepreneurial action. During the rural revitalization phase, the TTF has a broader scope for innovation

and entrepreneurship. This new phase requires us to address both market and governmental failures by incubating third-party (social) forces, moving beyond the provision of agricultural technologies to embrace holistic new business models that encompass cultural and creative output, digital tools, and more. In this era of business opportunity, the TTF needs to leverage digitalization, smart technologies, and big data to promote the fourth sector, while nurturing the high-value-added fifth sector through science-led innovation and the delivery of cultural and creative experiences, as expected by the new mainstream. The TTF is also expected to facilitate the integration of the primary, secondary, and tertiary sectors with an eco-agriculture paradigm. This integration plays a crucial role in the holistic development of urban and rural areas, marking a significant step towards rural revitalization.